The Big Book
of
American
Political
Quotations

Over 2,400 observations on America, Government,

Politics, Parties, Elections, and more

Compiled by

Kevin G. Barkes

This book is dedicated to my mother, who secured for me my first library card and first introduced me to ideas other than my own.

I love quotations because it is a joy to find thoughts one might have, beautifully expressed with much authority by someone recognized wiser than oneself.
-Marlene Dietrich

It should be noted that not all of the quotations listed herein are by or about America or Americans. Nonetheless, an argument can be made they are still applicable and, in fact, have been quoted by many American publications as relevant to the government and politics of the United States.

About the author:

Kevin G. Barkes is a software publishing system designer, blogger, and writer. An autodidact, he has been, in prior careers, a veterinary assistant; a newspaper reporter, photographer, and editor; a typesetter; a computer systems manager; a computer system and facility management consultant; a magazine columnist; a newspaper columnist; and a software support engineer.

He has been accumulating quotations for over 30 years; first, as ''fortune cookies'' for his computer bulletin board system, and then out of admiration of the brilliance of others.

He has two children, two grandchildren, a wife, and, as of this writing, three dogs, two cats, and Lucille, a transient wolf spider in his basement office.

Visit his daily blog, The KGB Report, at http://www.kgbreport.com. The KGB Report also features the KGB Quotations Database, containing over 40,000 quotations on all subjects.

Be alerted to upcoming publications or make comments on this one by emailing him at kgbarkes@gmail.com.

The typeset version of this book was produced by the author using the Datalogics DL Pager® automated batch composition system. Professional book typesetting services are available by contacting the author at the email address above.

The Big Book of American Political Quotations

A Conservative is a fellow who is standing athwart history yelling 'Stop,' at a time when no one is inclined to do so, or to have much patience with those who so urge it.
-William F. Buckley, Jr.

A Constitution of Government once changed from Freedom, can never be restored. Liberty, once lost, is lost forever.
-John Adams

A Democrat will plunge into a raging water to save a victim in distress. A Republican will stay on the shore and explain that it's really in the victim's best interest to save himself.
-Bob Levey

A Government protected by foreigners will never be accepted by a free people.
-Napoleon Bonaparte

A Libertarian is just a Republican who takes drugs.
-Bob Black

A President's hardest task is not to do what is right, but to know what is right.
-Lyndon B. Johnson

A ballot is like a bullet. You don't throw your ballots until you see a target, and if that target is not within your reach, keep your ballot in your pocket.
-Malcolm X

A black man voting for the Republicans makes about as much sense as a chicken voting for Colonel Sanders.
-Buddy Watts, Sr.

A bureaucrat is a Democrat who holds some office that a Republican wants.
-Alben W. Barkley

A candidate is a person who gets money from the rich and votes from the poor to protect them from each other.
-Stanislaw Lem

A certain kind of rich man afflicted with the symptoms of moral dandyism sooner or later comes to the conclusion that it isn't enough merely to make money. He feels obliged to hold views, to espouse causes and elect Presidents, to explain to a trembling world how and why the world went wrong. The spectacle is nearly always comic.
-Lewis H. Lapham

A choice between Democrats or Republicans is like a choice between paper or plastic.
-Kinky Friedman

A comedian wields more power than the most connected politician on Earth.
-Tommy Chong

A commonplace of political rhetoric has it that the quality of a civilization may be measured by how it cares for its elderly. Just as surely, the future of a society may be forecast by how it cares for its young.
-Daniel Patrick Moynihan

A compassionate conservative is someone who electrocutes juveniles but lets them have a last 'make a wish.'
-Garrison Keillor

A conservative government is an organized hypocrisy.
-Benjamin Disraeli

A conservative is a liberal who got mugged the night before.
-Frank Rizzo

A conservative is a man who is too cowardly to fight and too fat to run.
-Elbert Hubbard

A conservative is a man who wants the rules changed so no one can make a pile the way he did.
-Gregory Nunn

A conservative is a man with two perfectly good legs who, however, has never learned how to walk forward.
-Franklin Delano Roosevelt

A conservative is a person who lives in a past that never existed.
-Variously attributed

A conservative is someone who believes in reform. But not now.
-Mort Sahl

A conservative is someone who demands a square deal for the rich.
-David Frost

A country survives its legislation. That truth should not comfort the conservative nor depress the radical. For it means that public policy can enlarge its scope and increase its audacity, can try big experiments without trembling too much over the result. This nation could enter upon the most radical experiments and could afford to fail in them.
-Walter Lippmann

A decent and manly examination of the acts of government should be not only tolerated, but encouraged.
-*William Henry Harrison*

A democracy is a government in the hands of men of low birth, no property, and vulgar employments.
-*Aristotle*

A democracy is a place where numerous elections are held at great cost without issues and with interchangeable candidates.
-*Gore Vidal*

A democracy is peace-loving. It does not like to go to war. It is slow to rise to provocation. When it has once been provoked to the point where it must grasp the sword, it does not easily forgive its adversary for having produced this situation.
-*George F. Kennan*

A democracy must provide itself with a foil of its own and none is better or more effective than an aristocracy of intellect and service.
-*Nicholas Murray Butler*

A democracy needs an opposition, especially in time of war, precisely to keep the government honest, and to point to whatever errors (or possible errors) it finds in the government's actions.
-*Eugene Volokh*

A democracy survives when its citizens have access to trustworthy and impartial sources of information, when it can discern lies from truth. Take this away and a democracy dies.
-*Chris Hedges*

The Big Book of American Political Quotations

A democracy- that is a government of all the people, by all the people, for all the people; of course, a government of the principles of eternal justice, the unchanging law of God; for shortness' sake I will call it the idea of Freedom.
-*Theodore Parker*

A democratic government is the only one in which those who vote for a tax can escape the obligation to pay it.
-*Alexis de Tocqueville*

A dog is like a liberal. He wants to please everybody. A cat really doesn't need to know that everybody loves him.
-*William Kunstler*

A drunkard or a gambler may be weaned from his ways, but not a politician.
-*Anthony Trollope*

A fair degree of literacy of speech... is increasingly rare in politicians and not necessarily regarded as an asset.
-*Rae Foley*

A famous Frenchman once said, War has become far too important to entrust to the generals. Today, business, I think, should be saying: Politics have become far too important to entrust to the politicians.
-*Dwight D. Eisenhower*

A flea can be taught everything a congressman can.
-*Mark Twain*

A form of government that is not the result of a long sequence of shared experiences, efforts, and endeavors can never take root.
-*Napoleon Bonaparte*

The Big Book of American Political Quotations

A gaffe occurs not when a politician lies, but when he tells the truth.
-*Michael Kinsley*

A general dissolution of principles and manners will more surely overthrow the liberties of America than the whole force of the common enemy.
-*Samuel Adams*

A good American makes propaganda for whatever existence has forced him to become.
-*Saul Bellow*

A good politician is quite as unthinkable as an honest burglar.
-*H.L. Mencken*

A government and a society that silences those who dissent is one that has lost its way.
-*Henry Steele Commager*

A government is for the benefit of all the people.
-*William Howard Taft*

A government needs one hundred soldiers for every guerrilla it faces.
-*Fulgencio Batista*

A government that is big enough to give you all you want is big enough to take it all away.
-*Barry M. Goldwater*

A government which robs Peter to pay Paul can always depend on the support of Paul.
-*George Bernard Shaw*

The Big Book of American Political Quotations

A great democracy has got to be progressive, or it will soon cease to be either great or a democracy.
-Theodore Roosevelt

A group of politicians deciding to dump a President because his morals are bad is like the Mafia getting together to bump off the Godfather for not going to church on Sunday.
-Russell Baker

A hungry child knows no politics.
-Ronald Reagan

A just government maintains a healthy tension between the claims of authority and the claims of liberty.
-Russell Kirk

A lack of leadership is no substitute for inaction.
-Variously attributed

A large plural society cannot be governed without recognizing that, transcending its plural interests, there is a rational order with a superior common law.
-Walter Lippmann

A leader in the Democratic Party is a boss, in the Republican Party he is a leader.
-Harry S. Truman

A leader is one who, out of madness or goodness, volunteers to take upon himself the woe of the people. There are few men so foolish, hence the erratic quality of leadership in the world.
-John Updike

The Big Book of American Political Quotations

A leader takes people where they want to go. A great leader takes people where they don't necessarily want to go but ought to be.
-Rosalynn Carter

A leader who doesn't hesitate before he sends his nation into battle is not fit to be a leader.
-Golda Meir

A liberal is a conservative who's been arrested. A conservative is a liberal who's been mugged.
-Variously attributed

A liberal is a man or a woman or a child who looks forward to a better day, a more tranquil night, and a bright, infinite future.
-Leonard Bernstein

A liberal is a man too broadminded to take his own side in a quarrel.
-Robert Frost

A liberal is a person who believes that water can be made to run up-hill. A conservative is someone who believes everybody should pay for his water. I'm somewhere in between: I believe water should be free, but that water flows downhill.
-Theodore H. White

A liberal mind is a mind that is able to imagine itself believing anything.
-Max Eastman

A liberal society thrives on disagreement but is killed by dissension. Disagreement is the life blood of democracy, dissension is its cancer.
-Daniel J. Boorstin

A libertarian is someone who can believe that the police are no more than a gang of thugs without realizing that in the absence of police, thugs will gather into gangs.
-*S.M. Stirling*

A little government and a little luck are necessary in life; but only a fool trusts either of them.
-*P.J. O'Rourke*

A little righteous anger really brings out the best in the American personality. Our nation was born when 56 patriots got mad enough to sign the Declaration of Independence. We put a man on the moon because Sputnik made us mad at being number two in space. Getting mad in a constructive way is good for the soul- and the country.
-*Lee Iacocca*

A lot has been said about politics; some of it complimentary, but most of it accurate.
-*Eric Idle*

A lot of history is just dirty politics cleaned up for the consumption of children and other innocents.
-*Richard Reeves*

A lot of politicians manage to be important without being significant.
-*Kinky Friedman*

A low voter turnout is an indication of fewer people going to the polls.
-*Dan Quayle (vice president under George H.W. Bush)*

The Big Book of American Political Quotations

A man attains an elevated position only when his mediocrity prevents him from being a threat to others. And for this reason a democracy is never governed by the most competent, but rather by those whose insignificance will not jeopardize anyone else's self-esteem.
-Niccolò Machiavelli

A man cannot govern a nation if he cannot govern a city; he cannot govern a city if he cannot govern a family; he cannot govern a family unless he can govern himself; and he cannot govern himself unless his passions are subject to reason.
-Hugo Grotius

A man unwilling to bear his share of the burden of the government is unworthy to enjoy its blessings.
-William Jennings Bryan

A man who has both feet planted firmly in the air can be safely called a liberal as opposed to the conservative, who has both feet firmly planted in his mouth.
-Jacques Barzun

A man's admiration for absolute government is proportionate to the contempt he feels for those around him.
-Alexis de Tocqueville

A man who thinks of himself as belonging to a particular national group in America has not yet become an American.
-Woodrow Wilson

A modern democracy is a tyranny whose borders are undefined; one discovers how far one can go only by traveling in a straight line until one is stopped.
-Norman Mailer

A monarchy is the most expensive of all forms of government, the regal state requiring a costly parade, and he who depends on his own power to rule, must strengthen that power by bribing the active and enterprising whom he cannot intimidate.
-James Fenimore Cooper

A nation of sheep will beget a government of wolves.
-Edward R. Murrow

A patriot is mocked, scorned and hated; yet when his cause succeeds, all men will join him, for then it costs nothing to be a patriot.
-Mark Twain

A patriot must always be ready to defend his country against his government.
-Edward Abbey

A penny saved is a Congressional oversight.
-Variously attributed

A people can prosper under a very bad government and suffer under a very good one, if in the first case the local administration is effective and in the second it is inefficient.
-Annie Besant

A political convention is after all not a meeting of a corporation's board of directors; it is a fiesta, a carnival, a pig-rooting, horse-snorting, band-playing, voice-screaming medieval get-together of greed, practical lust, compromised idealism, career-advancement, meeting, feud, vendetta, conciliation, of rabble-rousers, fist fights (as it used to be), embraces, drunks (again as it used to be) and collective rivers of animal sweat.
-Norman Mailer

The Big Book of American Political Quotations

A political convention just is not a place where you can come away with any trace of faith in human nature.
-*Murray Kempton*

A political leader must keep looking over his shoulder all the time to see if the boys are still there. If they aren't still there, he's no longer a political leader.
-*Bernard Baruch*

A political organization is a transferable commodity. You could not find a better way of killing virtue than by packing it into one of these contraptions which some gang of thieves is sure to find useful.
-*John Jay Chapman*

A political problem thought of in military terms eventually becomes a military problem.
-*George C. Marshall*

A political society does not live to conduct foreign policy; it would be more correct to say that it conducts foreign policy in order to live.
-*George F. Kennan*

A politician is a guy who would lay down your life for his country.
-*Mary Louise Cecelia (Texas Guinan)*

A politician is a man who understands government, and it takes a politician to run a government. A statesman is a politician who's been dead 10 or 15 years.
-*Harry S. Truman*

A politician is an animal which can sit on a fence and yet keep both ears to the ground.
-*H.L. Mencken*

The Big Book of American Political Quotations

A politician is required to listen to humbug, talk humbug, condone humbug. The most we can hope is that we don't actually believe it.
-P.D. James

A politician should have three hats. One for throwing into the ring, one for talking through, and one for pulling rabbits out of if elected.
-Carl Sandburg

A politician will do anything to keep his job- even become a patriot.
-William Randolph Hearst

A politician's willingness to listen to good advice rises in inverse proportion to how badly he thinks he is doing.
-Pat Caddell

A politician's words reveal less about what he thinks about his subject than what he thinks about his audience.
-George F. Will

A politics that is not sensitive to the concerns and circumstances of people's lives, a politics that does not speak to and include people, is an intellectually arrogant politics that deserves to fail.
-Paul Wellstone

A popular Government without popular information, or the means of acquiring it, is but a Prologue to a Farce or a Tragedy, or perhaps both. Knowledge will forever govern ignorance: And a people who mean to be their own Governors, must arm themselves with the power which knowledge gives.
-James Madison

The Big Book of American Political Quotations

A power has risen up in the government greater than the people themselves, consisting of many and various and powerful interests, combined into one mass, and held together by the cohesive power of the vast surplus in the banks. (in 1836)
-*John C. Calhoun*

A professional politician is a professionally dishonorable man. In order to get anywhere near high office he has to make so many compromises and submit to so many humiliations that he becomes indistinguishable from a streetwalker.
-*H.L. Mencken*

A republic cannot succeed, till it contains a certain body of men imbued with the principles of justice and honor.
-*Charles Darwin*

A revolution requires of its leaders a record of unbroken infallibility; if they do not possess it, they are expected to invent it.
-*Murray Kempton*

A sensitive man is not happy as President. It is fight, fight, fight all the time.
-*Grover Cleveland*

A silent majority and government by the people is incompatible.
-*Tom Hayden*

A society is not 'free' merely because the freedoms the people are doing away with are those they voted at the last election to do without.
-*William F. Buckley, Jr.*

A society of sheep must in time beget a government of wolves.
-*Bertrand de Jouvenel*

14

A state is not a mere society, having a common place, established for the prevention of mutual crime and for the sake of exchange... Political society exists for the sake of noble actions, and not of mere companionship.
-Aristotle

A state without the means of some change is without the means of its conservation.
-Edmund Burke

A statesman is a successful politician who is dead.
-Thomas B. Reed

A statesman is any politician it's considered safe to name a school after.
-Bill Vaughan

A statesman makes the occasion, but the occasion makes the politician.
-G.S. Hilliard

A straw vote only shows which way the hot air blows.
-O. Henry

A system in which we may have an enforced rest from legislation for two years is not bad.
-William Howard Taft

A taxpayer is someone who has to work for the federal government without taking a civil-service test.
-Ronald Reagan

The Big Book of American Political Quotations

A thoughtful mind, when it sees a nation's flag, sees not the flag only, but the nation itself; and whatever may be its symbols, its insignia, he reads chiefly in the flag the government, the principles, the truths, the history which belongs to the nation that sets it forth.
-Henry Ward Beecher

A time will come when a politician who has willfully made war and promoted international dissension will be as sure of the dock and much surer of the noose than a private homicide. It is not reasonable that those who gamble with men's lives should not stake their own.
-H.G. Wells

A true patriot would keep the attention of his fellow citizens awake to their grievances, and not allow them to rest till the causes of their just complaints are removed.
-Samuel Adams

A true world outlook is incompatible with a foreign imperialism, no matter how high-minded the governing country.
-Wendell Willkie

A truly American sentiment recognizes the dignity of labor and the fact that honor lies in honest toil.
-Grover Cleveland

A typical vice of American politics is the avoidance of saying anything real on real issues.
-Theodore Roosevelt

A union of government and religion tends to destroy government and degrade religion.
-Hugo Black

The Big Book of American Political Quotations

A week is a long time in politics.
-Harold Wilson

A wise man distrusts his neighbor. A wiser man distrusts both his neighbor and himself. The wisest man of all distrusts his government.
-Taylor Caldwell

A zeal for different opinions concerning religion, concerning government, and many other points, as well of speculation as of practice; an attachment to different leaders ambitiously contending for pre-eminence and power; or to persons of other descriptions whose fortunes have been interesting to the human passions, have, in turn, divided mankind into parties, inflamed them with mutual animosity, and rendered them much more disposed to vex and oppress each other than to co-operate for their common good.
-James Madison

Advertising men and politicians are dangerous if they are separated. Together they are diabolical.
-Phillip Adams

After 6 o'clock we can be friends; but before 6, it's politics.
-Thomas P. (Tip) O'Neill

After each war there is a little less democracy to save.
-Brooks Atkinson

After four years at the United Nations I sometimes yearn for the peace and tranquility of a political convention.
-Adlai E. Stevenson II

All Fundamentalists are conservatives, but not all conservatives are Fundamentalists. The best conservatives can often give lessons to the liberals in true liberality of spirit, but the Fundamentalist program is essentially illiberal and intolerant.
-Harry Emerson Fosdick

All Presidents start out to run a crusade but after a couple of years they find they are running something less heroic and much more intractable: namely the presidency. The people are well cured by then of election fever, during which they think they are choosing Moses. In the third year, they look on the man as a sinner and a bumbler and begin to poke around for rumors of another Messiah.
-Alistair Cooke

All conservatives are such from personal defects. They have been effeminated by position or nature, born halt and blind, through luxury of their parents, and can only, like invalids, act on the defensive.
-Ralph Waldo Emerson

All government originates in families, and if neglected there, it will hardly exist in society... The foundation of all free government and of all social order must be laid in families and in the discipline of youth.
-Noah Webster

All governments suffer a recurring problem: Power attracts pathological personalities. It is not that power corrupts but that it is magnetic to the corruptible. Such people have a tendency to become drunk on violence, a condition to which they are quickly addicted.
-Frank Herbert

All great change in America begins at the dinner table.
-Ronald Reagan

All ideologies are idiotic, whether religious or political, for it is conceptual thinking, the conceptual word, which has so unfortunately divided man.
-*Jiddu Krishnamurti*

All issues are political issues, and politics itself is a mass of lies, evasions, folly, hatred, and schizophrenia.
-*George Orwell*

All of the great leaders have had one characteristic in common: it was the willingness to confront unequivocally the major anxiety of their people in their time. This, and not much else, is the essence of leadership.
-*John Kenneth Galbraith*

All of us who are concerned for peace and triumph or reason and justice must be keenly aware how small an influence reason and honest good will exert upon events in the political field.
-*Albert Einstein*

All of you, I am sure, have heard many cries about Government interference with business and about 'creeping socialism.' I should like to remind the gentlemen who make these complaints that if events had been allowed to continue as they were going prior to March 4, 1933, most of them would have no businesses left for the Government or for anyone else to interfere with- and almost surely we would have socialism in this country, real socialism. (in 1950)
-*Harry S. Truman*

All political parties die at last of swallowing their own lies.
-*John Arbuthnot*

All political power is primarily an illusion. Illusion. Mirrors and blue smoke, beautiful blue smoke rolling over the surface of highly polished mirrors, first a thin veil of blue smoke, then a thick cloud that suddenly dissolves into wisps of blue smoke, the mirrors catching it all, bouncing it back and forth.
-Jimmy Breslin

All politicians are humble, and seldom let you forget it. They go around the country boasting about their humility. They are proud of their humility. Many are downright arrogant about their humility and insist that it qualifies them to be President.
-Russell Baker

All politicians are to some extent salesmen.
-George F. Will

All politics are based on the indifference of the majority.
-James Reston

All politics is a matter of working hard without reward, or with a living wage for a time, in the hope of booty later.
-Ernest Hemingway

All politics is local.
-Thomas P. (Tip) O'Neill

All politics takes place on a slippery slope. The most important four words in politics are 'up to a point.'
-George F. Will

All presidents rail against the press. It goes with the turf.
-Helen Thomas

All that a good government aims at... is to add no unnecessary and artificial aid to the force of its own unavoidable consequences, and to abstain from fortifying and accumulating social inequality as a means of increasing political inequalities.
-*James Fenimore Cooper*

All that America can be proud of is a balanced cat diet.
-*Charles Chaplin*

All the perplexities, confusion and distress in America arise, not from defects in their Constitution or Confederation, not from want of honor or virtue, so much as from the downright ignorance of the nature of coin, credit and circulation.
-*John Adams*

All the President is, is a glorified public relations man who spends his time flattering, kissing and kicking people to get them to do what they are supposed to do anyway.
-*Harry S. Truman*

All the public business in Congress now connects itself with intrigues, and there is great danger that the whole government will degenerate into a struggle of cabals.
-*John Quincy Adams*

All the problems we face in the United States today can be traced to an unenlightened immigration policy on the part of the American Indian.
-*Pat Paulsen*

All those who seek to destroy the liberties of a democratic nation ought to know that war is the surest and shortest means to accomplish it.
-*Alexis de Tocqueville*

The Big Book of American Political Quotations

All truly great achievements in history resulted from the actualization of principles, not from the clever evaluation of political conditions.
-Henry Kissinger

All who have ever written on government are unanimous, that among a people generally corrupt, liberty cannot long exist.
-Edmund Burke

Allow the president to invade a neighboring nation, whenever he shall deem it necessary to repel an invasion, and you allow him to do so whenever he may choose to say he deems it necessary for such a purpose- and you allow him to make war at pleasure.
-Abraham Lincoln

Almost all propaganda is designed to create fear. Heads of governments and their officials know that a frightened people is easier to govern, will forfeit rights it would otherwise defend, is less likely to demand a better life, and will agree to millions and millions being spend on 'Defense.'
-J.B. Priestley

Almost always tradition is nothing but a record and a machine-made imitation of the habits that our ancestors created. The average conservative is a slave to the most incidental and trivial part of his forefathers' glory- to the archaic formula which happened to express their genius or the eighteenth-century contrivance by which for a time it was served.
-Walter Lippmann

Along with voting, jury duty, and paying taxes, goofing off is one of the central obligations of American citizenship.
-Sarah Vowell

Although He is regularly asked to do so, God does not take sides in American politics.
-*George Mitchell*

Although in our country the Chief Magistrate must almost of necessity be chosen by a party and stand pledged to its principles and measures, yet in his official action he should not be the President of a part only, but of the whole people of the United States.
-*James K. Polk*

Although it is not true that all conservatives are stupid people, it is true that most stupid people are conservative.
-*John Stuart Mill*

Always vote for principle, though you may vote alone, and you may cherish the sweetest reflection that your vote is never lost.
-*John Quincy Adams*

Am I embarrassed to speak for a less than perfect democracy? Not one bit. Find me a better one.
-*Daniel Patrick Moynihan*

Am I the only guy in this country who's fed up with what's happening? Where the hell is our outrage? We should be screaming bloody murder. We've got a gang of clueless bozos steering our ship of state right over a cliff, we've got corporate gangsters stealing us blind, and we can't even clean up after a hurricane much less build a hybrid car. But instead of getting mad, everyone sits around and nods their heads when the politicians say, 'Stay the Course.'
-*Lee Iacocca*

America did not invent human rights. In a very real sense, it is the other way around. Human rights invented America.
-*Jimmy Carter*

The Big Book of American Political Quotations

America goes not abroad in search of monsters to destroy. She is the well-wisher to freedom and independence of all. She is the champion and vindicator only of her own.
-John Quincy Adams

America has always been a country of amateurs where the professional, that is to say, the man who claims authority as a member of an élite which knows the law in some field or other, is an object of distrust and resentment.
-W.H. Auden

America has leapt from barbarism to decadence without touching civilization.
-John O'Hara

America has no permanent friends or enemies, only interests.
-Henry Kissinger

America has the laws and the material resources it takes to insure justice for all its people. What it lacks is the heart, the humanity...
-Shirley Chisholm

America is a country no one should go to for the first time.
-Jawaharlal Nehru

America is a country ready to be taken, in fact, longing to be taken by political leaders ready to restore democracy and trust to the political process.
-Arianna Huffington

America is a country that can choke on a gnat, or swallow tigers.
-Adlai E. Stevenson II

The Big Book of American Political Quotations

America is a country with a First Amendment, and you're allowed to publish just about anything you want, as long as it's not real secret information. Of course, nobody really does that except for, you know, you guys in the media.
-Tom Clancy

America is a democracy and has no Hitler, but I am afraid for her future; there are hard times ahead for the American people, troubles will be coming from within and without. America cannot smile away their Negro problem nor Hiroshima and Nagasaki. There are cosmic laws.
-Albert Einstein

America is a hurricane, and the only people who do not hear the sound are those fortunate if incredibly stupid and smug White Protestants who live in the center, in the serene eye of the big wind.
-Norman Mailer

America is a land of wonders, in which everything is in constant motion and every change seems an improvement.
-Alexis de Tocqueville

America is a land where a citizen will cross the ocean to fight for democracy- and won't cross the street to vote in a national election.
-Bill Vaughan

America is a large, friendly dog in a very small room. Every time it wags its tail, it knocks over a chair.
-Arnold J. Toynbee

America is a melting pot. The people at the bottom get burned while all the scum floats to the top.
-Charlie King

The Big Book of American Political Quotations

America is a passionate idea or it is nothing. America is a human brotherhood or it is a chaos.
-Max Lerner

America is a place where Jewish merchants sell Zen love beads to agnostics for Christmas.
-John Burton Brimer

America is a tune. It must be sung together.
-Gerald Stanley Lee

America is a vast conspiracy to make you happy.
-John Updike

America is a young country with an old mentality.
-George Santayana

America is an enormous frosted cupcake in the middle of millions of starving people.
-Gloria Steinem

America is another name for opportunity. Our whole history appears like a last effort of divine Providence in behalf of the human race.
-Ralph Waldo Emerson

America is at that awkward stage. It's too late to work within the system, but too early to shoot the bastards.
-Claire Wolfe

America is Elvis Presley- the most beautiful, talented, rebellious nation in the history of Earth. And now, you're in your Vegas years. You've squeezed yourself into a white jumpsuit, you're wheezing your way through 'Love Me Tender' and you might be about to pass away bloated on the toilet. But you're still the King.
-John Oliver

America is hope. It is compassion. It is excellence. It is valor.
-Paul Tsongas

America is like an unfaithful lover who promised us more than we got.
-Charlotte Bunch

America is neither free nor brave, but a land of tight, iron-clanking little wills, everybody trying to put it over everybody else, and a land of men absolutely devoid of the real courage of trust, trust in life's sacred spontaneity. They can't trust life until they can control it.
-D.H. Lawrence

America is not a land of money but of wealth- not a land of rich people, but of successful workers.
-Henry Ford

America is not a melting pot. It is a sizzling cauldron.
-Barbara Mikulski

America is not Europe. America was created as an escape from, and antidote to, Europe.
-Michael Kelly

The Big Book of American Political Quotations

America is not just a power, it is a promise. It is not enough for our country to be extraordinary in might; it must be exemplary in meaning.
-Nelson Rockefeller

America is so vast that almost everything said about it is likely to be true, and the opposite is probably equally true.
-James T. Farrell

America is still a government of the naive, for the naive, and by the naive. He who does not know this, nor relish it, has no inkling of the nature of his country.
-Christopher Morley

America is the best half-educated country in the world.
-Nicholas Murray Butler

America is the greatest of opportunities and the worst of influences.
-George Santayana

America is the land of wide lawns and narrow minds.
-Ernest Hemingway

America is the land where people are free to dream whatever they want, so long as that dream doesn't make Midwesterners feel icky.
-Lewis Black

America is the most inventive country in the world because everybody has access to information.
-Tom Clancy

The Big Book of American Political Quotations

America is the only country in the world that's still in the business of making bombs that can end the world and TV shows that make it seem like a good idea.
-Bill Maher

America is the only country in the world where businessmen get together over twenty dollar steaks to discuss hard times.
-Honey Greer

America is the only country in the world where you can suffer culture shock without leaving home.
-Florence King

America is the only country where a significant proportion of the population believes that professional wrestling is real but the moon landing was faked.
-David Letterman

America is the only nation in history which miraculously has gone directly from barbarism to degeneration without the usual interval of civilization.
-Georges Clemenceau

America is the sum of all our journeys as we search for our national community and our national culture.
-Paul Tsongas

America isn't young, you know. It's ancient and evil. With aluminum siding.
-Rudy Rucker

America is where the wildest humans on the planet came to do anything they damn pleased.
-P.J. O'Rourke

America lives in the heart of every man everywhere who wishes to find a region where he will be free to work out his destiny as he chooses.
-*Woodrow Wilson*

America makes prodigious mistakes, America has colossal faults, but one thing cannot be denied: America is always on the move. She may be going to Hell, of course, but at least she isn't standing still.
-*E.E. Cummings*

America needs fewer men obsessed with erecting fences of hate, suspicion and name calling.
-*William Arthur Ward*

America of the future will be all malls connected by interstates. All because your parents no longer can their own tomatoes.
-*Garrison Keillor*

America stands strongest in challenging terrorism when we do not give up an inch of our civil liberties.
-*Dennis Kucinich*

America was born of revolt, flourished on dissent, became great through experimentation.
-*Henry Steele Commager*

America was not built by conformists, but by mutineers.
-*Jim Hightower*

America is where the wildest humans on the planet came to do anything they damn pleased.
-*P.J. O'Rourke*

America will tolerate the taking of a human life without giving it a second thought. But don't misuse a household pet.
-*Dick Gregory*

America's a family. We all yell at each other. It all works out.
-*Louis C.K.*

America's always been a great place to be crazy. It just used to be harder to make a living that way.
-*Charles Pierce*

America's greatest days are ahead of us and America's greatest days are behind us. The problem is right now, and always has been.
-*Stephen Colbert*

America's greatest enemy is not from without, but from within, and that enemy is hate: hatred of races, peoples, classes and religions. If America ever dies, it will be not through conquest but suicide.
-*Fulton J. Sheen*

America's health care system is neither healthy, caring, nor a system.
-*Walter Cronkite*

America's one of the finest countries anyone ever stole.
-*Bobcat Goldwaith*

America's two great specialties are demagogues and rock and roll, and we've all heard plenty of both in our time.
-*Stephen King*

America's vulnerability comes precisely from its strength, its wealth, its power and its modernity. It's the usual story of the dog chasing its own tail.
-*Oriana Fallaci*

The Big Book of American Political Quotations

America, my friends, is the only country in the world actually founded on liberty- the only one. People went to America to be free.
-Margaret Thatcher

America, where overnight success is both a legend and a major industry.
-John Leggett

America, where thanks to Congress, there are forty million laws to enforce the Ten Commandments.
-Anatole France

America, which has the most glorious present still existing in the world today, hardly stops to enjoy it, in her insatiable appetite for the future.
-Anne Morrow Lindbergh

America... is the only country where the failure to promote yourself is widely considered arrogant.
-Garry Trudeau

America... It is a fabulous country, the only fabulous country; it is the only place where miracles not only happen, but where they happen all the time.
-Thomas Wolfe

America... just a nation of two hundred million used car salesmen with all the money we need to buy guns and no qualms about killing anybody else in the world who tries to make us uncomfortable.
-Hunter S. Thompson

America: Race riots, fascist police, AND THE BEST DAMNED ICE CREAM IN THE WORLD!
-(Button, circa 1968)

American capitalism is predatory, and American politics are corrupt: The same thing is true in England and the same in France; but in all these three countries the dominating fact is that whatever the people get ready to change the government, they can change it.
-*Upton Sinclair*

American cities are like badger holes ringed with trash.
-*John Steinbeck*

American college students are like American colleges; each has half-dulled faculties.
-*James Thurber*

American critics are like American universities. They both have dull and half-dead faculties.
-*Edward Albee*

American democracy must be a failure because it places the supreme authority in the hands of the poorest and most ignorant part of the society.
-*Thomas Babington Macaulay*

American English is essentially British English without the redundancies, including the monarchy.
-*Ivan C. Amaya*

American high school graduates are among the most sensitive illiterates in the world.
-*Allan Bloom*

American humor... is not subtle. It is something that makes you laugh the moment you hear it, you have not to think a scrap.
-*Elinor Glyn*

The Big Book of American Political Quotations

American husbands are the best in the world; no other husbands are so generous to their wives, or can be so easily divorced.
-*Elinor Glyn*

American journalism is a class institution, serving the rich and spurning the poor.
-*Upton Sinclair*

American men, as a group, seem to be interested in only two things, money and breasts. It seems a very narrow outlook.
-*Hedy Lamarr*

American patriotism is generally something that amuses Europeans, I suppose because children look idiotic saluting the flag and because the constitution contains so many cracks through which the lawyers may creep.
-*Katherine Whitehorn*

American political opportunities are heavily loaded against those who are simultaneously intelligent and honest.
-*Richard Dawkins*

American politics used to be an amateur sport. But somewhere along the way, we handed over to professionals all the things people used to do for free.
-*Bob Schieffer*

American public opinion is like an ocean- it cannot be stirred by a teaspoon.
-*Hubert H. Humphrey*

American society is a sort of flat, freshwater pond which absorbs silently, without reaction, anything which is thrown into it.
-*Henry Adams*

American society to me and my brother was thrilling because, first of all, the food made noise. We were so excited about Rice Krispies and Coca-Cola. We had only silent food in our country, and we loved listening to our lunch and breakfast.
-*Mike Nichols*

Americanism is a question of principle, of purpose, of idealism, of character. It is not a matter of birthplace or creed or line of descent.
-*Theodore Roosevelt*

Americanism: Using money you haven't earned to buy things you don't need to impress people you don't like.
-*Robert Quillen*

Americans are a broad-minded people. They'll accept the fact that a person can be alcoholic, a dope fiend or a wife-beater, but if a man doesn't drive a car, everybody thinks that something is wrong with him.
-*Art Buchwald*

Americans are apocalyptic by nature. The reason why is that we've always had so much, so we live in deadly fear that people are going to take it away from us.
-*Stephen King*

Americans are apt to be unduly interested in discovering what average opinion believes average opinion to be; and this national weakness finds its nemesis in the stock market.
-*John Maynard Keynes*

Americans are benevolently ignorant about Canada, while Canadians are malevolently well informed about the United States.
-*J. Bartlett Brebner*

The Big Book of American Political Quotations

Americans are fat all year round, but the holidays are when we really hit our stride. And you can bet the food we eat will be just as unhealthy as the families we're forced to visit.
-Lewis Black

Americans are like a rich father who wishes he knew how to give his sons the hardships that made him rich.
-Robert Frost

Americans are optimists. They hope they'll be wealthy someday- and they're positive they can get one more brushful of paint out of an empty can.
-Bernard Williams

Americans are overreachers; overreaching is the most admirable of the many American excesses.
-George F. Will

Americans are pragmatic, relatively uncomplicated, hearty and given to broad humor.
-Herb Caen

Americans are so enamored of equality, they would rather be equal in slavery than unequal in freedom.
-Alexis de Tocqueville

Americans are so tensed and keyed up that it's impossible even to put them to sleep with a sermon.
-Norman Vincent Peale

Americans are willing to go to enormous trouble and expense defending their principles with arms, very little trouble and expense advocating them with words.
-E.B. White

Americans believe that freedom was their invention. They have been known to send peace-corps troops to Athens to teach the Greeks the meaning of democracy.
-*Peter Ustinov*

Americans detest all lies except lies spoken in public or printed lies.
-*E.W. Howe*

Americans don't want leadership. They want alchemy.
-*Michael Kinsley*

Americans have a tendency to think the problem with politics lies with their candidates and not themselves. The truth is Americans deserve the blame for the state of our politics and the state of our media.
-*Jonah Goldberg*

Americans have always been able to handle austerity and even adversity. Prosperity is what is doing us in.
-*James Reston*

Americans have an abiding belief in their ability to control reality by purely material means... airline insurance replaces the fear of death with the comforting prospect of cash.
-*Cecil Beaton*

Americans have gotten the message that life is easier if they don't think straight.
-*Florence King*

Americans have no capacity for abstract thought, and make bad coffee.
-*Georges Clemenceau*

The Big Book of American Political Quotations

Americans have one of the greatest legal systems, but not a monopoly of the sense of justice, which is universal; nor have we a permanent copyright on the means of securing justice, for it is the spirit and not the form of law that keeps justice alive.
-*Earl Warren*

Americans learn only from catastrophes and not from experience.
-*Theodore Roosevelt*

Americans love a winner. Americans will not tolerate a loser. Americans despise cowards. Americans play to win all of the time.
-*George S. Patton, Jr.*

Americans love spending money, whether they have it or not.
-*David Wyss*

Americans make money by playing 'money games,' namely mergers, acquisitions, by simply moving money back and forth... instead of creating and producing goods with some actual value.
-*Akito Morita*

Americans must be the most sententious people in history. Far too busy to be religious, they have always felt that they sorely needed guidance.
-*Saul Bellow*

Americans never quit.
-*Douglas MacArthur*

Americans now read Facebook more than the Bible. I guess nobody wants to read about a guy who could only come up with 12 friends.
-*Conan O'Brien*

Americans think of themselves collectively as a huge rescue squad on twenty-four-hour call to any spot on the globe where dispute and conflict may erupt.
-Eldridge Cleaver

Americans took a great deal too much credit for creating wealth, when most of the time they had really just been living off natural bounty unprecedented in the history of the world.
-Jane Smiley

Americans treat history like a cookbook. Whenever they are uncertain what to do next, they turn to history and look up the proper recipe, invariably designated 'the lesson of history.'
-Russell Baker

Americans used to roar like lions for liberty. Now we bleat like sheep for security.
-Norman Vincent Peale

Americans want to be protected, but not at the cost of vitiating the values that make us Americans.
-Maureen Dowd

Americans will buy anything, as long as it doesn't cross the thin line between cute and demonic.
-Ian Shoales

Americans will listen, but they do not care to read. War and Peace must wait for the leisure of retirement, which never really comes: meanwhile it helps to furnish the living room.
-Anthony Burgess

Americans will put up with anything provided it doesn't block traffic.
-Dan Rather

Americans... still believe in an America where anything's possible-they just don't think their leaders do.
-*Barack Obama*

Among all the world's races, some obscure Bedouin tribes possibly apart, Americans are the most prone to misinformation. This is not the consequence of any special preference for mendacity, although at the higher levels of their public administration that tendency is impressive. It is rather that so much of what they themselves believe is wrong.
-*John Kenneth Galbraith*

Among Republicans, family values seems to be an article of faith, like heaven, rather than an actual way of life.
-*John Bonnano*

Among politicians and businessman, Pragmatism is the current term for 'To hell with our children.'
-*Edward Abbey*

An American cannot converse, but he can discuss, and his talk falls into a dissertation. He speaks to you as if he was addressing a meeting; and if he should chance to become warm in the discussion, he will say Gentlemen to the person with whom he is conversing.
-*Alexis de Tocqueville*

An 'American tradition' is anything that happened to a baby boomer twice.
-*Randall Munroe*

An American who can make money, invoke God, and be no better than his neighbor, has nothing to fear but truth itself.
-*Marya Mannes*

An Independent is someone who wants to take the politics out of politics.
-Adlai E. Stevenson II

An aristocracy in a republic is like a chicken whose head has been cut off; it may run about in a lovely way, but in fact it's dead.
-Nancy Mitford

An educated, healthy and confident nation is harder to govern.
-Ernest Benn

An election is a bet on the future, not a popularity test of the past.
-James Reston

An election is coming. Universal peace is declared, and the foxes have a sincere interest in prolonging the lives of the poultry.
-George Eliot

An ex-President practicing law or going into business is like a locomotive hauling a delivery wagon. He has lost his sense of proportion. The concerns of other people and even his own affairs seem to small to be worth bothering about.
-Grover Cleveland

An honest politician is one who, when he is bought, will stay bought.
-Simon Cameron

An imbalance between rich and poor is the oldest and most fatal ailment of all republics.
-Plutarch

An infinite God ought to be able to protect himself, without going in partnership with State Legislatures. Certainly he ought not so to act that laws become necessary to keep him from being laughed at. No one thinks of protecting Shakespeare from ridicule, by the threat of fine and imprisonment.
-*Robert G. Ingersoll*

Ancient Rome declined because it had a Senate; now what's going to happen to us with both a Senate and a House?
-*Will Rogers*

And a democracy can't exist without free speech and the right to assemble. And that's what Americans tend to forget. And they're born into a culture where they take all of their freedoms for granted.
-*Larry Flynt*

And above all, above all, honest work must be rewarded by a fair and just tax system. The tax system today does not reward hard work: it penalizes it. Inherited or invested wealth frequently multiplies itself while paying no taxes at all. But wages on the assembly line or in farming the land, these hard-earned dollars are taxed to the very last penny.
-*George McGovern*

And by the way, I've about had it with this 'greatest generation' malarkey. You people have one stock market crash in 1929, and it takes you a dozen years to go get a job. Then you wait until Germany and Japan have conquered half the world before it occurs to you to get involved in World War II. After that you get surprised by a million Red Chinese in Korea. Where do you put a million Red Chinese so they'll be a surprise? You spend the entire 1950s watching Lawrence Welk and designing tail fins. You come up with the idea for Vietnam. Thanks. And you elect Richard Nixon. The hell with you.
-*P.J. O'Rourke*

And political parties, overanxious for vote catching, become tolerant to intolerant groups.
-Wendell Willkie

And who can suffer injury by just taxation, impartial laws and the application of the Jeffersonian doctrine of equal rights to all and special privileges to none? Only those whose accumulations are stained with dishonesty and whose immoral methods have given them a distorted view of business, society and government. Accumulating by conscious frauds more money than they can use upon themselves, wisely distribute or safely leave to their children, these denounce as public enemies all who question their methods or throw a light upon their crimes.
-William Jennings Bryan

Any American who is prepared to run for president should automatically, by definition, be disqualified from ever doing so.
-Gore Vidal

Any big organization can be subverted by governments or multinational special interests. They have the resources to cast doubt and fear over any group they feel threatened by.
-Arlo Guthrie

Any company executive who overcharges the government more than $5 million will be fined $50 or have to go to traffic school three nights a week.
-Art Buchwald

Any country with 'democratic' in the title, isn't.
-Variously attributed

Any man who does not like dogs and want them about does not deserve to be in the White House.
-*Calvin Coolidge*

Any government has as much of a duty to avoid war as a ship's captain has to avoid a shipwreck.
-*Guy de Maupassant*

Any government which made the welfare of men depend on the character of their governors was an illusion.
-*Daniel J. Boorstin*

Any people anywhere being inclined and having the power have the right to rise up and shake off the existing government, and form a new one that suits them better.
-*Abraham Lincoln*

Any political picture can be changed to suit the needs of the powers that be.
-*Thor Heyerdahl*

Any sufficiently advanced coup is indistinguishable from an election.
-*John Alejandro King (The Covert Comic)*

Any time you find the government involved in a conspiracy to violate the citizenship or the civil rights of a people, then you are wasting your time going to that government expecting redress.
-*Malcolm X*

Anybody has a right to evade taxes if he can get away with it. No citizen has a moral obligation to assist in maintaining the government.
-*J.P. Morgan*

Anybody who wants the presidency so much that he'll spend two years organizing and campaigning for it is not to be trusted with the office.
-David Broder

Anyone who tells you they enjoy running in a campaign for public office is either crazy or lying to you.
-Barney Frank

Anyone wishing to communicate with Americans should do so by e-mail, which has been specially invented for the purpose, involving neither physical proximity nor speech.
-Auberon Waugh

Anything anybody can say about America is true.
-Emmett Grogan

Anything that's strange is no good to the average American. If it doesn't have Chicago plumbing, it's nonsense.
-Ray Bradbury

Applause, mingled with boos and hisses, is about all that the average voter is able or willing to contribute to public life.
-Elmer Davis

Are the people who run for president really the best in a country of 240 million? If so, something has happened to the gene pool.
-Bob McKenzie

Are you a politician or does lying just run in your family?
-Fannie Flagg

Are you aware that the candidate is known all over Washington as a shameless extrovert? Not only that, but this man is reliably reported to have practiced nepotism with his sister-in-law and he has a sister who was once a thespian in New York. He matriculated with co-eds at the University, and it is an established fact that before his marriage he habitually practiced celibacy. (attributed; campaign speech against Claude Pepper)
-George Smathers

Aristocracy is the spirit of the Old Testament, democracy of the New.
-Napoleon Bonaparte

Arizona is the meth lab of democracy.
-Jon Stewart

As an American, I naturally spend most of my time laughing.
-H.L. Mencken

As I would not be a slave, so I would not be a master. This expresses my idea of democracy. Whatever differs from this, to the extent of the difference, is no democracy.
-Abraham Lincoln

As a human rights issue, the effort to end violence against women becomes a government's obligation, not just a good idea.
-Charlotte Bunch

As a practical matter, property is whatever the government allows you to keep.
-Jerry Pournelle

As a rule, large capitalists are Republicans and small capitalists are Democrats, but workingmen must remember that they are all capitalists, and that the many small ones, like the fewer large ones, are all politically supporting their class interests, and this is always and everywhere the capitalist class.
-Eugene V. Debs

As against the 'invisible hand' of Adam Smith, there has to be a visible hand of politicians whose objective is to have the kind of society that is caring and humane.
-Pierre Elliott Trudeau

As an organized political group, the Communists have done nothing to damage our society a fraction as much as what their enemies have done in the name of defending us against subversion.
-Murray Kempton

As democracy is perfected, the office of president represents, more and more closely, the inner soul of the people. On some great and glorious day the plain folks of the land will reach their heart's desire at last and the White House will be adorned by a downright moron.
-H.L. Mencken

As for the Republicans- how can one regard seriously a frightened, greedy, nostalgic huddle of tradesmen and lucky idlers who shut their eyes to history and science, steel their emotions against decent human sympathy, cling to sordid and provincial ideals exalting sheer acquisitiveness and condoning artificial hardship for the non-materially-shrewd, dwell smugly and sentimentally in a distorted dream-cosmos of outmoded phrases and principles and attitudes based on the bygone agricultural-handicraft world, and revel in (consciously or unconsciously) mendacious assumptions (such as the notion that real liberty is synonymous with the single detail of unrestricted economic license or that a rational planning of resource-distribution would contravene some vague and mystical 'American heritage'...) utterly contrary to fact and without the slightest foundation in human experience? Intellectually, the Republican idea deserves the tolerance and respect one gives to the dead.
-*H.P. Lovecraft*

As free citizens in a political democracy, we have a responsibility to be interested and involved in the affairs of the human community, be it at the local or the global level.
-*Paul Wellstone*

As freedom is the only safeguard of governments, so are order and moderation generally necessary to preserve freedom.
-*Thomas Babington Macaulay*

As individuals and as a nation, we now suffer from social narcissism. The beloved Echo of our ancestors, the virgin America, has been abandoned. We have fallen in love with our own image, with images of our making, which turn out to be images of ourselves.
-*Daniel J. Boorstin*

As many as six out of ten American adults have never read a book of any kind, and the bulletins from the nation's educational frontiers read like the casualty reports from a lost war.
-*Lewis H. Lapham*

As long as judges tinker with the Constitution to 'do what the people want,' instead of what the document actually commands, politicians who pick and confirm new federal judges will naturally want only those who agree with them politically.
-*Antonin Scalia*

As long as mankind shall continue to bestow more liberal applause on their destroyers than on their benefactors, the thirst of military glory will ever be the vice of the most exalted characters.
-*Edward Gibbon*

As long as politics is the shadow cast on society by big business, the attenuation of the shadow will not change the substance.
-*John Dewey*

As long as you continue to tar social democracy with all the crimes of communism, I feel equally entitled to tar the free market with the crimes of slavery, segregation, colonialism and genocide; piss me off and I'll add fascism and the Nazis.
-*Greg Erwin*

As my father once explained to me, our 'rights' are only as strong as the democracy that protects them. Because we are a people's democracy here in America, as great as the people of this country can be, but also as fallible, we must stay ever vigilant in the face of any 'tyranny' of the majority, no matter the stated objective.
-*George Takei*

As one digs deeper into the national character of the Americans, one sees that they have sought the value of everything in this world only in the answer to this single question: how much money will it bring in?

-Alexis de Tocqueville

As people do better, they start voting like Republicans... unless they have too much education and vote Democratic, which proves there can be too much of a good thing.

-Karl Rove

As religion is imitated and mocked by hypocrisy, so public duty is parodied by patriotism.

-J. E. Thorold Rogers

As societies grow decadent, the language grows decadent, too. Words are used to disguise, not to illuminate, action: you liberate a city by destroying it. Words are to confuse, so that at election time people will solemnly vote against their own interests.

-Gore Vidal

As someone who is not Christian, it is hard for me to believe Christians are a persecuted people in America... maybe, God willing, one of you will rise up and get to be President of this country. Or maybe 44. In a row.

-Jon Stewart

As the United States is the freest of all nations, so, too, its people sympathize with all people struggling for liberty and self-government; but while so sympathizing it is due to our honor that we should abstain from enforcing our views upon unwilling nations and from taking an interested part, without invitation,.

-Ulysses S. Grant

As the master politician navigates the ship of state, he both creates and responds to public opinion. Adept at tacking with the wind, he also succeeds, at times, in generating breezes of his own.
-*Stewart Udall*

As the only class distinction available in a democracy, the college degree has created a caste society as rigid as ancient India's.
-*Florence King*

As to my political faith- I have never voted. My father was a Democrat, my mother a Republican, and I am an Episcopalian.
-*George C. Marshall*

Ask a man which way he is going to vote, and he will probably tell you. Ask him, however, why, and vagueness is all.
-*Bernard Levin*

At a time when politics deals in distortions and half truths, truth is to be found in the liberal arts.
-*Joyce Carol Oates*

At the bottom of all patriotism there is war: that is why I am no patriot.
-*Jules Renard*

At the core, the American citizen soldiers knew the difference between right and wrong, and they didn't want to live in a world in which wrong prevailed. So they fought, and won, and we all of us, living and yet to be born, must be forever profoundly grateful.
-*Stephen Ambrose*

At the heart of all political movements the concept of the basic inequality of man was enthroned and practiced, and the skill of politicians consisted in how cleverly they hid this elementary truth and gained votes by pretending the contrary.
-*Richard Nathaniel Wright*

At the White House, everybody works for the same person. They're all part of the same company. But on Capitol Hill, they're all independent contractors. They all work for themselves. That's a formula for getting news.
-*Bob Schieffer*

At this late stage in the history of American capitalism I'm not sure I know how much testimony still needs to be presented to establish the relation between profit and theft.
--*Lewis H. Lapham*

At times it seems that the media have become the mainstream culture in children's lives. Parents have become the alternative. Americans once expected parents to raise their children in accordance with the dominant cultural messages. Today they are expected to raise their children in opposition to it.
-*Ellen Goodman*

Automation and technology would be a great boon if it were creative, if there were more leisure, more opportunity to engage in raising a family, providing guidance to the young, all the stuff we say we need. America will work if we're all in it together. It'll work when there's a shared sense of destiny. It can be done!
-*Jerry Brown*

Backward is just not a natural direction for Americans to look- historical ignorance remains a national characteristic.
-*Larry McMurtry*

Bad officials are elected by good citizens who do not vote.
-*George Jean Nathan*

Be a freethinker. One reason our politics is so screwed up is because everyone has become so tribal. As you go down the path of life, ask what's true, not who else believes it.
-*Bill Maher*

Be thankful we're not getting all the government we're paying for.
-*Will Rogers*

Because man and woman are the complement of one another, we need woman's thought in national affairs to make a safe and stable government.
-*Elizabeth Cady Stanton*

Because of cutbacks in civic education from the 1970s onward, ... two-thirds of Americans today don't even know that their country has three branches of government... so they don't know whom to hold accountable for the country's festering problems. What I worry about is that when problems are not addressed, people will not know who is responsible, and when the problems get bad enough- another serious terrorist attack, another financial meltdown- some one person will come forward and say, 'Give me total power, and I will solve this problem.' That is how the Roman republic fell... That is how democracy dies. And if something is not done to improve the level of civic knowledge, that is what you should worry about at night.
-*David Souter (former Supreme Court Justice)*

Beer commercials are so patriotic: 'Made the American Way.' What does that have to do with America? Is that what America stands for? Feeling sluggish and urinating frequently?
-*Scott Blakeman*

Behind the ostensible government sits enthroned an invisible government owing no allegiance and acknowledging no responsibility to the people. To destroy this invisible government, to befoul the unholy alliance between corrupt business and corrupt politics is the first task of the statesmanship of today.
-*Theodore Roosevelt*

Behold a republic standing erect while empires all around are bowed beneath the weight of their own armaments- a republic whose flag is loved while other flags are only feared.
-*William Jennings Bryan*

Being American is not a matter of birth. We must practice it every day, lest we become something else.
-*Malcolm Wallop*

Being a liberal is the best thing on earth you can be.
-*Lauren Bacall*

Being a politician is a poor profession. Being a public servant is a noble one.
-*Herbert Hoover*

Being against torture ought to be sort of a bipartisan thing.
-*Karl Lehenbauer*

Being conservative is a way of being skeptic.
-*Jorge Luis Borges*

Being elected to Congress is regarded as being sent on a looting raid for one's friends.
-*George F. Will*

The Big Book of American Political Quotations

Being in politics is like being a football coach. You have to be smart enough to understand the game and dumb enough to think it's important.
-Eugene McCarthy

Being in Washington is more fictional than being in Hollywood.
-George Lucas

Being president is like being a jackass in a hailstorm. There's nothing to do but to stand there and take it.
-Lyndon B. Johnson

Being president is like running a cemetery: you've got a lot of people under you and nobody's listening.
-Bill Clinton

Besides the danger of a direct mixture of religion and civil government, there is an evil which ought to be guarded against in the indefinite accumulation of property from the capacity of holding it in perpetuity by ecclesiastical corporations.
-James Madison

Better the occasional faults of a Government that lives in a spirit of charity than the consistent omissions of a Government frozen in the ice of its own indifference.
-Franklin Delano Roosevelt

Beware the politically obsessed. They are often bright and interesting, but they have something missing in their natures; there is a hole, an empty place, and they use politics to fill it up. It leaves them somehow misshapen.
-Peggy Noonan

Blind faith in your leaders, or in anything, will get you killed.
-Bruce Springsteen

Both the strength and the weakness of American democracy is in the fact that it's a true people's democracy, and it can be as great as the people can be, but it's also as fallible as the people are.
-George Takei

Brain-dead activities are national pastimes in America and other developed countries- an intellectual abdication that cannot be accomplished on the Internet.
-Mario Sanchez

Building democracy as an imposition from abroad is a form of imperialism.
-Lech Walesa

Building weapons that we don't need, don't work, and aren't necessary, and have no mission- that's not bad politics, that's robbery.
-Paul Newman

Bumper-sticker patriotism is no way to honor our veterans.
-Aaron Sorkin

Bureaucracy is not an obstacle to democracy but an inevitable complement to it.
-Joseph A. Schumpeter

But America is a great, unwieldy Body. Its Progress must be slow. It is like a large Fleet sailing under Convoy. The fleetest Sailors must wait for the dullest and slowest.
-John Adams

But this is the great danger America faces. That we will cease to be one nation and become instead a collection of interest groups: city against suburb, region against region, individual against individual. Each seeking to satisfy private wants.
-Barbara Jordan

But there is one way in this country in which all men are created equal- there is one human institution that makes a pauper the equal of a Rockefeller, the stupid man the equal of an Einstein, and the ignorant man the equal of any college president. That institution, gentlemen, is a court. It can be the Supreme Court of the United States or the humblest J.P. court in the land, or this honorable court which you serve. Our courts have their faults, as does any human institution, but in this country our courts are the great levellers, and in our courts all men are created equal.
-Harper Lee

But what is Government itself, but the greatest of all reflections on human nature?
-James Madison

But with Congress- every time they make a joke it's a law. And every time they make a law it's a joke.
-Will Rogers

By any precise definition, Washington is a city of advanced depravity. There one meets and dines with the truly great killers of the age, but only the quirkily fastidious are offended, for the killers are urbane and learned gentlemen who discuss their work with wit and charm and know which tool to use on the escargots.
-Russell Baker

By 'radical,' I understand one who goes too far; by 'conservative,' one who does not go far enough; by 'reactionary,' one who won't go at all.
-*Woodrow Wilson*

By definition, a government has no conscience. Sometimes it has a policy, but nothing more.
-*Albert Camus*

By giving the government unlimited powers, the most arbitrary rule can be made legal; and in this way a democracy may set up the most complete despotism imaginable.
-*Friedrich Hayek*

By sending the contradictory message that the famous are just plain folks on Mount Olympus, America has forged a relentless tension between loftiness and accessibility. Stir in the fact that the inborn talent and intelligence needed to achieve fame are immune to distributive tinkering by government programs and you have a definition of fame certain to produce envious rage: somebody screwed democracy.
-*Florence King*

Call me an optimist, but I believe our government will come up with a totally unsatisfactory solution to a completely unnecessary crisis.
-*Andy Borowitz*

Campaign promises are- by long democratic tradition- the least binding form of human commitment.
-*Antonin Scalia*

Can any of you seriously say the Bill of Rights could get through Congress today? It wouldn't even get out of committee.
-*F. Lee Bailey*

Capital, n. The seat of misgovernment.
-Ambrose Bierce

Celebrity distorts democracy by giving the rich, beautiful, and famous more authority than they deserve.
-Maureen Dowd

Censorship is advertising paid by the government.
-Frederico Fellini

Censorship must be done by the government or it's not censorship.
-Penn Jillette

Children are the universal scapegoats for any political agenda.
-Variously attributed

Children in school are not students, they are pupils. It is typical of certain kinds of politicians that they should regard children as adults, the better subsequently, and consequently, to regard adults as children.
-Theodore Dalrymple

Chinks in America's egalitarian armor are not hard to find. Democracy is the fig leaf of elitism.
-Florence King

Christmas is a time when kids tell Santa what they want and adults pay for it. Deficits are when adults tell the government what they want and their kids pay for it.
-Richard Lamm

Churches are becoming political organizations... It probably will not be long until the churches will divide as sharply upon political, as upon theological questions; and when that day comes, if there are not liberals enough to hold the balance of power, this Government will be destroyed. The liberty of man is not safe in the hands of any church. Wherever the Bible and sword are in partnership, man is a slave.
-Robert G. Ingersoll

Citizens by birth or choice of a common country, that country has a right to concentrate your affections.-The name of AMERICAN, which belongs to you, in your national capacity, must always exalt the just pride of Patriotism, more than any appellation derived from local discriminations.
-George Washington

Citizenship is no light trifle to be jeopardized any moment Congress decides to do so under the name of one of its general or implied grants of power.
-Hugo Black

Civics is not only how to run the country before it's your turn to run the country; it is, in fact, the study of power, practical political power. And you must start that process at an age level when kids' brains are still open and malleable.
-Richard Dreyfuss

Civil government, so far as it is instituted for the security of property, is in reality instituted for the defense of the rich against the poor, or of those who have some property against those who have none at all.
-Adam Smith

Civility is not not saying negative or harsh things. It is not the absence of critical analysis. It is the manner in which we are sharing this territorial freedom of political discussion. If our discourse is yelled and screamed and interrupted and patronized, that's uncivil.
-Richard Dreyfuss

Come senators, congressmen
Please heed the call
Don't stand in the doorway
Don't block up the hall
For he that gets hurt
Will be he who has stalled
There's a battle outside and it is ragin'
It'll soon shake your windows and rattle your walls
For the times they are a-changin'.
-Bob Dylan

Come, come, my conservative friend, wipe the dew off your spectacles, and see that the world is moving.
-Elizabeth Cady Stanton

Comedians and politicians each tell the audience what it wants to hear. The difference is that the audience laughs at the comedian and the politician laughs at the audience.
-Alexis A. Gilliland

Communism is a hateful thing and a menace to peace and organized government; but the communism of combined wealth and capital, the outgrowth of overweening cupidity and selfishness, which insidiously undermines the justice and integrity of free institutions, is not less dangerous than the communism of oppressed poverty and toil, which, exasperated by injustice and discontent, attacks with wild disorder the citadel of rule.
-Grover Cleveland

Communists worship the Devil himself. Socialists believe damnation is a good system run by bad people. And liberals want to send everyone to hell because it's warm there in the winter.
-P.J. O'Rourke

Computers aren't for voting: they're for picking up underage girls. Voting by computer sounds really cool and futuristic- if this were 1969.
-Bill Maher

Conceit, arrogance and egotism are the essentials of patriotism. Let me illustrate. Patriotism assumes that our globe is divided into little spots, each one surrounded by an iron gate. Those who have had the fortune of being born on some particular spot consider themselves nobler, better, grander, more intelligent than those living beings inhabiting any other spot. It is, therefore, the duty of everyone living on that chosen spot to fight, kill and die in the attempt to impose his superiority upon all the others.
-Emma Goldman

Congress acknowledged that society's accumulated myths and fears about disability and disease are as handicapping as are the physical limitations that flow from actual impairment.
-William J. Brennan, Jr.

Congress is continually appointing fact-finding committees, when what we really need are some fact-facing committees.
-Roger Allen

Congress is so beholden to the money that any solution in the general interest will be frustrated and subverted by the corporate interests who feel they will be damaged by progress, fair play and justice.
-E.L. Doctorow

Congress is so strange. A man gets up to speak and says nothing. Nobody listens- and then everybody disagrees.
-Boris Marshalov

Congress no longer declares war or makes budgets. So that's the end of the constitution as a working machine.
-Gore Vidal

Congress seems drugged and inert most of the time. Even when the problems it ignores build up to crises and erupt in strikes, riots, and demonstrations, it has not moved. Its idea of meeting a problem is to hold hearings or, in extreme cases, to appoint a commission.
-Shirley Chisholm

Congress: Bingo with billions.
-Red Skelton

Congress: the legislative stone in America's urethra.
-Jon Stewart

Congressional responsibility. It's like saying Fukushima Sushi.
-Will Durst

Congressmen are a palm-pounding pack of preening pols.
-William Safire

Conscience reigns but it does not govern.
-Paul Valery

Consensus is the negation of leadership.
-Margaret Thatcher

Conservatism Inc. always has to appeal to nationalism and populism to win elections. However, the point is that they didn't actually mean it- it was simply a way to get the rubes to vote Republican.
-*James Kirkpatrick*

Conservatism discards Prescription, shrinks from Principle, disavows Progress; having rejected all respect for antiquity, it offers no redress for the present, and makes no preparation for the future.
-*Benjamin Disraeli*

Conservatism is less a set of ideas than it is a pathological distemper, a militant anger over the fact that the universe is not closed and life is not static.
-*Bill Moyers*

Conservatism is only as good as what it conserves.
-*Friedrich Hayek*

Conservatism is the policy of making no changes and consulting your grandmother when in doubt.
-*Woodrow Wilson*

Conservatism, though a necessary element in any stable society, is not a social program; in its paternalistic, nationalistic and power adoring tendencies it is often closer to socialism than true liberalism; and with its traditionalistic, anti-intellectual, and often mystical propensities it will never, except in short periods of disillusionment, appeal to the young and all those others who believe that some changes are desirable if this world is to become a better place.
-*Friedrich Hayek*

Conservative, n. A statesman enamored of existing evils, as opposed to a Liberal, who wants to replace them with others.
-*Ambrose Bierce*

Conservatives are afraid the public will not understand, liberals are afraid the public will understand.
-*Dick Armey*

Conservatives are more religious than liberals- although there is no evidence that they're nicer people because of it.
-*Andy Rooney*

Conservatives define themselves in terms of what they oppose.
-*George F. Will*

Conservatives have historically seen people falling through the cracks in society and said that's the way things work, survival of the fittest. Liberals see people falling through the cracks and say we've got to do something about those people falling through the cracks so we need a strong government that can provide programs and assist those people. Populists say there shouldn't be any cracks, let's fix them.
-*Jim Hightower*

Conservatives haven't had a new idea since they began purchasing women in lieu of clubbing them.
-*Rack Jite*

Conservatives in particular shouldn't lament our dim and doubtful foresight of what lies ahead. It is, after all, the condition of human freedom.
-*William Kristol*

Conservatives pride themselves on resisting change, which is as it should be. But intelligent deference to tradition and stability can evolve into intellectual sloth and moral fanaticism, as when conservatives simply decline to look up from dogma because the effort to raise their heads and reconsider is too great.
-*William F. Buckley, Jr.*

Conservatives say if you don't give the rich more money, they will lose their incentive to invest. As for the poor, they tell us they've lost all incentive because we've given them too much money.
-George Carlin

Conservatives- or better, pro-corporate apologists- hijacked the vocabulary of Jeffersonian liberalism and turned words like 'progress,' 'opportunity,' and 'individualism' into tools for making the plunder of America sound like divine right.
-Bill Moyers

Corrupt citizens breed corrupt rulers, and it is the mob who finally decides when virtue shall die.
-Taylor Caldwell

Corrupted by wealth and power, your government is like a restaurant with only one dish. They've got a set of Republican waiters on one side and a set of Democratic waiters on the other side. But no matter which set of waiters brings you the dish, the legislative grub is all prepared in the same Wall Street kitchen.
-Huey P. Long

Corruption is nature's way of restoring our faith in democracy.
-Peter Ustinov

Corruption is no stranger to Washington; it is a famous resident.
-Walter Goodman

Counterpart to the knee-jerk liberal is the new knee-pad conservative, always groveling before the rich and powerful.
-Edward Abbey

Creative semantics is the key to contemporary government; it consists of talking in strange tongues lest the public learn the inevitable inconveniently early.
-*George F. Will*

Crime is contagious. If the government becomes a lawbreaker, it breeds contempt for law; it invites every man to become a law unto himself; it invites anarchy.
-*Louis Brandeis*

Cruel leaders are replaced only to have new leaders turn cruel.
-*Che Guevara*

Cutting down our democratic protections to get at the enemy is profoundly dumb. We end up doing the enemy's work for them, and from within.
-*Amanda Vanstone*

Cynically defined, a libertarian is a person who believes that all humans should live in total and absolute submission to market forces, at all times from birth to death, without any chance of escape.
-*Paul Treanor*

Dad, as a good American, believed his newspapers.
-*Upton Sinclair*

Debate on public issues should be uninhibited, robust, and wide-open, and that it may well include vehement, caustic, and sometimes unpleasantly sharp attacks on government and public officials.
-*William J. Brennan, Jr.*

Debt is the fatal disease of all republics, the first thing and the mightiest to undermine governments and corrupt the people.
-*Wendell Phillips*

Decency, security, and liberty alike demand that government officials shall be subjected to the same rules of conduct that are commands to the citizen.
-Louis Brandeis

Decisions are made by those who show up. Don't ever forget that you're a citizen of this world.
-Aaron Sorkin

Democracies are indeed slow to make war, but once embarked upon a martial venture are equally slow to make peace and reluctant to make a tolerable, rather than a vindictive, peace.
-Reinhold Neibuhr

Democracy and socialism are means to an end, not the end itself.
-Jawaharlal Nehru

Democracy becomes a government of bullies tempered by editors.
-Ralph Waldo Emerson

Democracy can withstand ideological attacks if democracy will provide earnestly and liberally for the welfare of its people.
-Omar Bradley

Democracy cannot consist solely of elections that are nearly always fictitious and managed by rich landowners and professional politicians.
-Che Guevara

Democracy cannot survive without the guidance of a creative minority.
-Harlan F. Stone

Democracy consists of choosing your dictators, after they've told you what you think it is you want to hear.
-Alan Coren

Democracy demands that all of its citizens begin the race even. Egalitarianism insists that they all finish even.
-Roger Price

Democracy demands that elected members be able to realize fully the role for which they have been chosen.
-Pierre Elliott Trudeau

Democracy demands that little men should not take big ones too seriously; it dies when it is full of little men who think they are big themselves.
-C.S. Lewis

Democracy does not guarantee equality of conditions- it only guarantees equality of opportunity.
-Irving Kristol

Democracy encourages the majority to decide things about which the majority is ignorant.
-John Simon

Democracy gives every man the right to be his own oppressor.
-James Russell Lowell

Democracy has to be born anew every generation, and education is its midwife.
-John Dewey

Democracy is a device that ensures we shall be governed no better than we deserve.
-George Bernard Shaw

Democracy is a form of government in which it is permitted to wonder aloud what the country could do under first-class management.
-Doug Larson

Democracy is a genus, not a species. Getting a democracy is rather like getting a 'mammal' for a gift. Kittens are nice. Wolverines will lunch on your eyeballs. You don't drop a wolverine in your friend's lap, and then walk away feeling you've done him a favor, since 'the best pets are mammals.'
-Will Wilkinson

Democracy is a pathetic belief in the collective wisdom of individual ignorance.
-H.L. Mencken

Democracy is a political method, that is to say, a certain type of institutional arrangement for arriving at political- legislative and administrative- decisions and hence incapable of being an end in itself.
-Joseph A. Schumpeter

Democracy is a small hard core of common agreement, surrounded by a rich variety of individual differences.
-James Bryant Conant

Democracy is also a form of worship. It is the worship of jackals by jackasses.
-H.L. Mencken

Democracy is an abuse of statistics.
-Jorge Luis Borges

Democracy is an experiment, and the right of the majority to rule is no more inherent than the right of the minority to rule; and unless the majority represents sane, righteous, unselfish public sentiment, it has no inherent right.
-*William Allen White*

Democracy is an objective. Democratization is a process. Democratization serves the cause of peace because it offers the possibility of justice and of progressive change without force.
-*Boutros-Boutros Ghali*

Democracy is based upon the conviction that there are extraordinary possibilities in ordinary people.
-*Harry Emerson Fosdick*

Democracy is being allowed to vote for the candidate you dislike least.
-*Robert Byrne*

Democracy is finding proximate solutions to insoluble problems.
-*Reinhold Neibuhr*

Democracy is fine by me, but sometimes I'm not sure about you. (song lyrics)
-*Garrison Keillor*

Democracy is good. I say this because other systems are worse. So we are forced to accept democracy. It has good points and also bad. But merely saying that democracy will solve all problems is utterly wrong. Problems are solved by intelligence and hard work.
-*Jawaharlal Nehru*

Democracy is like a raft. It won't sink, but you'll always have your feet wet.
-*Russell B. Long*

Democracy is like a tambourine- not everyone can be trusted with it.
-*John Oliver*

Democracy is mob rule, but with income taxes.
-*Variously attributed*

Democracy is more cruel than wars or tyrants.
-*Lucias Annaeus Seneca*

Democracy is more vindictive than Cabinets. The wars of peoples will be more terrible than those of kings.
-*Winston Churchill*

Democracy is no harlot to be picked up in the street by a man with a tommy gun.
-*Winston Churchill*

Democracy is something that you must learn each generation. It has to be taught.
-*Anthony Kennedy*

Democracy is still upon its trial. The civic genius of our people is its only bulwark.
-*William James*

Democracy is that which affords a rule of living as well as a test of faith.
-*Jane Addams*

Democracy is the art and science of running the circus from the monkey cage.
-*H.L. Mencken*

Democracy is the crude leading the crud.
-*Florence King*

Democracy is the name we give to the people when we need them.
-*Robert Pelleve*

Democracy is the only system that persists in asking the powers that be whether they are the powers that ought to be.
-*Sydney J. Harris*

Democracy is the process by which people choose the man who'll get the blame.
-*Bertrand Russell*

Democracy is the recurrent suspicion that more than half of the people are right more than half of the time.
-*E.B. White*

Democracy is the theory that the people know what they want, and deserve to get it good and hard.
-*H.L. Mencken*

Democracy is the worst form of government except all those other forms that have been tried from time to time.
-*Winston Churchill*

Democracy is timelessly human, and timelessness always implies a certain amount of potential youthfulness.
-*Thomas Mann*

Democracy is too good to share with just anybody.
-Nigel Rees

Democracy is, by the nature of it, a self-canceling business; and it gives in the long run a net result of zero.
-Thomas Carlyle

Democracy may become frenzied, but it has feelings and can be moved. As for aristocracy, it is always cold and never forgives.
-Napoleon Bonaparte

Democracy may not prove in the long run to be as efficient as other forms of government, but it has one saving grace: it allows us to know and say that it isn't.
-Bill Moyers

Democracy means government by discussion, but it is only effective if you can stop people talking.
-Clement Attlee

Democracy means government by the uneducated, while aristocracy means government by the badly educated.
-G.K. Chesterton

Democracy means rule by the majority... and the majority is always wrong. The only comfort I can find lies in the thought that the majority of today represents the opinions of the minority of yesterday. Democracy will always be twenty years behind its time.
-A.S. Neill

Democracy means that if the doorbell rings in the early hours, it is likely to be the milkman.
-Winston Churchill

Democracy means that people can say what they want to. All the people. It means that they can vote as they wish. All the people. It means that they can worship God in any way they feel right, and that includes Christians and Jews and voodoo doctors as well. It means that everybody should have a job, if he's willing to work, and an education, and the right to bring up his children without fear of the future. And it means that the old shall be provided for, without shame to themselves or to their families. It means do unto others as you would have others do unto you. It also means the prayers of the pilgrim fathers in the wilderness, and the Declaration of Independence, and the Constitution of the United States, and the Bill of Rights, and the Emancipation Proclamation, and the dreams of an immigrant mother for her children. And that's what I believe in.
-Dalton Trumbo

Democracy means the belief that humanistic culture should prevail.
-John Dewey

Democracy must be rooted in a rational philosophy that first and foremost recognizes the right of an individual.
-Terry Goodkind

Democracy must be something more than two wolves and a sheep voting on what to have for dinner.
-James Bovard

Democracy simply means the bludgeoning of the people by the people for the people.
-Oscar Wilde

Democracy substitutes election by the incompetent many for appointment by the corrupt few.
-George Bernard Shaw

Democracy without respect for individual rights sucks. It's just ganging up against the weird kid, and I'm always the weird kid.
-Penn Jillette

Democracy, like any non-coercive relationship, rests on a shared understanding of limits.
-Elizabeth Drew

Democrats believe people are basically good but must be saved from themselves by the government. Republicans believe people are basically bad but they'll be okay if they're left alone.
-Andy Rooney

Democrats get impeached for having sex. Republicans get impeached for undermining the integrity of the Republic.
-Kevin G. Barkes

Democrats will only become acceptable once they are comfortable in their minority status. Any farmer will tell you that certain animals run around and are unpleasant, but when they've been fixed, then they are happy and sedate.
-Grover Norquist

Despotism subjects a nation to one tyrant; democracy, to many.
-Marguerite Gardiner (Countess of Blessington)

Did you ever notice that when a politician does get an idea he usually gets it all wrong?
-Don Marquis

Diplomacy, n. The patriotic art of lying for one's country.
-Ambrose Bierce

Disbelief in magic can force a poor soul into believing in government and business.
-Tom Robbins

Discussion in America means dissent.
-James Thurber

Dishonesty in government is the business of every citizen.... It is not enough to do your own job. There's no particular virtue in that. Democracy isn't a gift. It's a responsibility.
-Dalton Trumbo

Divine right went out with the American Revolution and doesn't belong to the White House aides. What meat do they eat that makes them grow so great?
-Samuel J. Ervin

Do not seek to stop progress; do not seek to put the hand of politics on these scientific men who are doing a great work.
-Fiorello LaGuardia

Do not... regard the critics as questionable patriots. What were Washington and Jefferson and Adams but profound critics of the colonial status quo?
-Adlai E. Stevenson II

Do you ever get the feeling that the only reason we have elections is to find out if the polls were right?
-Robert Orben

Do you know what White House correspondents call actors who pose as reporters? Anchors.
-Jay Leno

Do you not know, my son, with how little wisdom the world is governed?
-Axel Oxenstierna (1583-1654)

Does politics have to be injected into everything?
-Sargent Shriver

Domestic policy can only lose elections. Foreign policy can kill us.
-John F. Kennedy

Don't buy a single vote more than necessary. I'll be damned if I'm going to pay for a landslide.
-Joseph P. Kennedy, Sr.

Don't expect other nations to have a democracy like ours- they don't have enough lawyers.
-Cullen Hightower

Don't get mad. Don't get even. Just get elected, then get even.
-James Carville

Don't vote. It only encourages them.
-Variously attributed

During a political campaign everyone is concerned with what a candidate will do on this or that question if he is elected except the candidate; he's too busy wondering what he'll do if he isn't elected.
-Everett Dirksen

During an election campaign the air is full of speeches and vice versa.
-Henry Adams

During the mid-1980s dairy farmers decided there was too much cheap milk at the supermarket. So the government bought and slaughtered 1.6 million dairy cows. How come the government never does anything like this with lawyers?
-*P.J. O'Rourke*

Economic law is not suppressed by legislated law.
-*Armen Alchian*

Economics dominates politics- and with that domination comes different forms of ruthlessness.
-*Chris Hedges*

Economy is the bone, politics is the flesh,
watch who they beat and who they eat.
-*Marge Piercy*

Education and democracy have the same goal: the fullest possible development of human capabilities.
-*Paul Wellstone*

Education is our only political safety. Outside of this ark all is deluge.
-*Horace Mann*

Education makes people easy to lead, but difficult to drive; easy to govern, but impossible to enslave.
-*Henry Peter Brougham*

Education remains the key to both economic and political empowerment.
-*Barbara Jordan*

Eighty percent of Republicans are just Democrats who don't know what's going on.
-Robert F. Kennedy, Jr.

Either one lives 'for' politics or one lives 'off' politics.
-Max Weber

Elected office holds more perks than Elvis' nightstand.
-Dennis Miller

Elected officials should be limited to two terms: one in office and one in prison.
-Kinky Friedman

Election year is that period when politicians get free speech mixed up with cheap talk.
-J.B. Kidd

Elections are a Western jerk-off.
-John le Carré

Elections are won by men and women chiefly because most people vote against somebody rather than for somebody.
-Franklin P. Adams

Elections give the illusion of freedom but are in fact a game among the powers that be, this is why we talk of 'formal democracy.' Instead of drawing forth the best energies of a people, this legal institution hands actual control to very different forces, turning democracy into another form of oligarchy and dictatorship.
-Karl Jaspers

Eliminate government waste no matter how much it costs.
-Variously attributed

Embrace the flag, and hope to someday live in that free republic for which it stands.
-*Variously attributed*

Engineering is the implementation of science; politics is the implementation of faith.
-*Marc Stiegler*

Envy is the basis of democracy.
-*Bertrand Russell*

Envy is the central fact of American life.
-*Gore Vidal*

Establishing lasting peace is the work of education; all politics can do is keep us out of war.
-*Maria Montessori*

Europe was created by history. America was created by philosophy.
-*Margaret Thatcher*

Even a liberal reporter is a patriot, wants the best for this country. And people, your fair and balanced friends at Fox, don't fully understand that.
-*Mike Wallace*

Even a purely moral act that has no hope of any immediate and visible political effect can gradually and indirectly, over time, gain in political significance.
-*Vaclav Havel*

Even though counting heads is not an ideal way to govern, at least it beats breaking them.
-*Learned Hand*

Even when conservatives have all the marbles, they still act as if they're under siege. Now that they are under siege, it is no time for them to act as if they're losing their marbles.
-*Maureen Dowd*

Eventually, somebody is going to be a hero, and somebody's going to be president. Not necessarily the same person.
-*Howard Baker, Jr.*

Ever occur to you why some of us can be this much concerned with animals suffering? Because government is not. Why not? Animals don't vote.
-*Paul Harvey*

Every American election summons the individual voter to weigh the past against the future.
-*Theodore H. White*

Every age that has historical status is governed by aristocracies.
-*Joseph Goebbels*

Every country has the government it deserves.
-*Joseph de Maistre*

Every decent man is ashamed of the government he lives under.
-*H.L. Mencken*

Every economy exists, no matter what the level of democracy, has elements of crony capitalism. It's- given human nature and given the democratic structures, which we all, I assume, adhere to, that is an inevitable consequence.
-*Alan Greenspan*

Every effort to confine Americanism to a single pattern, to constrain it to a single formula, is disloyalty to everything that is valid in Americanism.
-Henry Steele Commager

Every election is a sort of advance auction sale of stolen goods.
-H.L. Mencken

Every four years in the presidential election, some new precedent is broken.
-Nate Silver

Every government is a parliament of whores. The trouble is, in a democracy, the whores are us.
-P.J. O'Rourke

Every government is run by liars and nothing they say should be believed.
-I.F. Stone

Every guy looks in his pocket and then votes.
-Will Rogers

Every law is an evil, for every law is an infraction of liberty: And I repeat that government has but a choice of evils...
-Jeremy Bentham

Every new baby is a blind desperate vote for survival: people who find themselves unable to register an effective political protest against extermination do so by a biological act.
-Lewis Mumford

Every political good carried to the extreme must be productive of evil.
-*Mary Shelley*

Every politician is entitled to privacy, but no politician is entitled to hypocrisy.
-*Barney Frank*

Every politician should have been born an orphan and remain a bachelor.
-*Lady Bird Johnson*

Every politician we have, liberal or conservative, who gets caught drinking or chasing women is thrown out of office. It's backwards. It's more dangerous to have a clean-living President with his finger on the button. He thinks he's going right to heaven. You want to feel safe with a leader? Give me a guy who fights in bars and cheats on his wife. This is a man who wants to put off Judgment Day as long as possible.
-*Larry Miller*

Every post is honorable in which a man can serve his country.
-*George Washington*

Every president needs to deal with the permanent government of the country, and the permanent government of the country is Wall Street oligarchs and corporate plutocrats and the questions becomes what is the relationship between that president and Wall Street.
-*Cornel West*

Every tax, however, is to the person who pays it a badge, not of slavery but of liberty. It denotes that he is a subject to government, indeed, but that, as he has some property, he cannot himself be the property of a master.
-*Adam Smith*

Every time I think I'm a Republican they do something greedy, and every time I think I'm a Democrat, they do something stupid.
-*Jay Leno*

Every time government attempts to handle our affairs, it costs more and the results are worse than if we had handled them ourselves.
-*Benjamin Constant*

Every time you spend money, you're casting a vote for the kind of world you want.
-*Anna Lappe*

Everybody believes in democracy until he reaches the White House.
-*Thomas Cronin*

Everybody in America is soft, and hates conflict. The cure for this, both in politics and social life, is the same- hardihood. Give them raw truth.
-*John Jay Chapman*

Everybody keeps calling for Excellence- excellence not just in schooling, throughout society. But as soon as somebody or something stands out as Excellent, the other shout goes up: 'Elitism!' And whatever produced that thing, whoever praises that result, is promptly put down. 'Standing out' is undemocratic.
-*Jacques Barzun*

Everybody now seems to be talking about democracy. I don't understand this. As I think of it, democracy isn't like a Sunday suit to be brought out and worn only for parades.
-*Dalton Trumbo*

Everybody says not enough people vote. Now, I don't know nothing, but after the midterms, pretty obvious to me, that too many people vote.
-*Will Durst*

Everyone knows if a Republican comes out of the closet and sees a gay shadow, it means six more years of a Democratic administration.
-*Jon Stewart*

Everything begins in mysticism and ends in politics.
-*Charles Peguy*

Everything government touches turns to crap.
-*Ringo Starr*

Everything in our political life tends to hide from us that there is anything wiser than our ordinary selves.
-*Matthew Arnold*

Everything is politics.
-*Thomas Mann*

Experience should teach us to be most on our guard to protect liberty when the Government's purposes are beneficent. Men born to freedom are naturally alert to repel invasion of their liberty by evil-minded rulers. The greatest dangers to liberty lurk in insidious encroachment by men of zeal, well-meaning but without understanding.
-*Louis Brandeis*

Failure is not disgrace. It's just a pitch that you missed, and you'd better get ready for the next one. The next one might be the shot heard round the world. My son and I are Americans, we prepare for glory by failing until we don't.
-*Craig Ferguson*

Fanaticism displays itself in the masses; but the masses were rarely fanaticized; and the crimes ascribed to it were commonly due to the calculations of dispassionate politicians.
-*John Dalberg-Acton*

Fear is in almost all cases a wretched instrument of government, and ought in particular never to be employed against any order of men who have the smallest pretensions to independency.
-*Adam Smith*

Fear is the foundation of most governments; but it is so sordid and brutal a passion, and renders men in whose breasts it predominates so stupid and miserable, that Americans will not be likely to approve of any political institution which is founded on it.
-*John Adams*

Feeling good about government is like looking on the bright side of any catastrophe. When you quit looking on the bright side, the catastrophe is still there.
-*P.J. O'Rourke*

Few men have virtue to withstand the highest bidder.
-*George Washington*

Few people are prepared to use their reason without fear or favor, or bold enough to apply it relentlessly to every moral, political and social issue: to kings and ministers, to men in high places... And if we don't, we're doomed to remain mediocre.
-*Nicolas Chamfort*

Few things are more damaging to our democracy than a military officer who doesn't have the moral courage to stand up for what's right or the moral fiber to step aside when circumstances dictate.
-*Michael Mullen*

Fifty-one percent of a nation can establish a totalitarian regime, suppress minorities and still remain democratic.
-*Erik von Kuehnelt-Leddihn*

Finally, it occurs to me that the biggest problem with our elections is that however you vote, you wind up electing a politician.
-*Burt Prelutsky*

Finishing second in the Olympics gets you silver. Finishing second in politics gets you oblivion.
-*Richard M. Nixon*

Fire, water and government know nothing of mercy.
-*Variously attributed*

First Amendment freedoms are most in danger when the government seeks to control thought or to justify its laws for that impermissible end. The right to think is the beginning of freedom, and speech must be protected from the government because speech is the beginning of thought.
-*Anthony Kennedy*

Florida's number three industry, behind tourism and skin cancer, is voter fraud.
-*Dave Barry*

Football strategy does not originate in a scrimmage: it is useless to expect solutions in a political campaign.
-*Walter Lippmann*

For a politician to complain about the press is like a ship's captain complaining about the sea.
-*Enoch Powell*

For any twentieth-century American who'd been paying attention at all, the phrase 'criminal justice system' should have been warning enough.
-*L. Neil Smith*

For every action there is an equal and opposite government program.
-*Bob Wells*

For legislators make the citizens good by forming habits in them, and this is the wish of every legislator, and those who do not effect it miss their mark, and it is in this that a good constitution differs from a bad one.
-*Aristotle*

For most Americans the Constitution had become a hazy document, cited like the Bible on ceremonial occasions but forgotten in the daily transactions of life.
-*Arthur Schlesinger, Jr.*

For the First Amendment rests upon the premise that both religion and government can best work to achieve their lofty aims if each is left free from the other within its respective sphere.
-Hugo Black

For the first time in history, the human species as a whole has gone into politics. Everyone is in the act, and there is no telling what may come of it.
-Saul Bellow

For the most part our leaders are merely following out in front; they do but marshal us the way that we are going.
-Bergen Evans

For the sake of democracy, vigorous, civilized debate must replace the law of silence that political correctness has imposed.
-Theodore Dalrymple

For who can endure a doctrine which would allow only dentists to say whether our teeth were aching, only cobblers to say whether our shoes hurt us, and only governments to tell us whether we were being well governed?
-C.S. Lewis

Forms of government are forged mainly in the fire of practice, not in the vacuum of theory. They respond to national character and to national realities.
-George F. Kennan

Frankly, I don't mind not being President. I just mind that someone else is.
-Edward Kennedy

Frankly, I'd like to see the government get out of war altogether and leave the whole field to private industry.
-*Joseph Heller*

Free elections, a free press and an independent judiciary mean little when the free market means they are on sale to the highest bidder.
-*Arundhati Roy*

Free government is self-government. A government of the people by the people. The best government of this sort is that which the people think best.
-*Walter Bagehot*

Free trade, one of the greatest blessings which a government can confer on a people, is in almost every country unpopular.
-*Thomas Babington Macaulay*

Freedom has many flaws and our democracy is imperfect, but we have never had to put up a wall to keep our people in.
-*John F. Kennedy*

Freedom is not a supplier who delivers goods to our door. Democracy does not ensure that anything is accomplished- certainly not an economic miracle.
-*Karl Popper*

Freedom is when the people can speak, democracy is when the government listens.
-*Alasdair Farrugia*

Freedom of expression gives the essential democratic opportunity, but self-restraint is the essential civic discipline.
-*Charles Evans Hughes*

Freedom of opinion can only exist when the government thinks itself secure.
-*Bertrand Russell*

Freedom was given to humanity by God. But, governments, if they can help it, never give freedom. They just hand out slavery with slogans.
-*Taylor Caldwell*

Generals aren't in the business of commenting on the correctness or incorrectness of the President's decisions. Anybody who thinks he should be able to do that ought to be fired on the spot.
-*H. Norman Schwartzkopf, Jr.*

Generosity has built America. When we fail to invest in children, we have to pay the cost.
-*Bob Keeshan (Captain Kangaroo)*

George Washington's brother, Lawrence, was the Uncle of Our Country.
-*George Carlin*

Get all the fools on your side and you can be elected to anything.
-*Frank Dane*

Get yourself a spouse. Some things you just can't blame on the media or the government.
-*David Mahoney*

Give a member of Congress a junket and a mimeograph machine and he thinks he is secretary of state.
-*Dean Rusk*

Given a choice between two bald political candidates, the American people will vote for the less bald of the two.
-*Vic Gold*

Given the choice between a Republican and someone who acts like a Republican, people will vote for the real Republican all the time.
-*Harry S. Truman*

Giving every man a vote has no more made men wise and free than Christianity has made them good.
-*H.L. Mencken*

Giving money and power to government is like giving whiskey and car keys to teenage boys.
-*P.J. O'Rourke*

God is a politician; so is the devil.
-*Carrie Nation*

God is watching us. If we support someone we don't believe in and say he's electable, then God will make sure he's not elected and hope we do better the next time.
-*Mort Sahl*

Good government is no substitute for self-government.
-*Mohandas K. Gandhi*

Good government is the outcome of private virtue.
-*John Jay Chapman*

Government breaks your legs and then gives you a pair of crutches.
-*Rob Moody*

Government cannot provide values to persons who have none, or who have lost those they had. It cannot provide inner peace. It can provide outlets for moral energies, but it cannot create those energies.
-*Daniel Patrick Moynihan*

Government exists to protect us from each other. Where government has gone beyond its limits is in deciding to protect us from ourselves.
-*Ronald Reagan*

Government expands to absorb revenue- and then some.
-*Tom Wicker*

Government has no right to hurt the hair of an Atheist for his Opinions. Let him have a care of his Practices.
-*John Adams*

Government in America has taken on a vast mass of new duties and responsibilities; it has spread out its powers until they penetrate to every act of the citizen, however secret; it has begun to throw around its operations the high dignity and impeccability of religion; its agents become a separate and superior caste, with authority to bind and loose, and their thumbs in every pot. But it still remains, as it was in the beginning, the common enemy of all well-disposed, industrious and decent men. (in 1926)
-*H.L. Mencken*

Government is a contrivance of human wisdom to provide for human wants. Men have a right that these wants should be provided for by this wisdom.
-*Edmund Burke*

Government is a disease masquerading as its own cure.
-*Robert LeFevre*

Government is always religion applied to economics.
-*R.E. McMaster*

Government is an association of men who do violence to the rest of us.
-*Leo Tolstoy*

Government is an inescapable disease of human beings.
-*Robert A. Heinlein*

Government is contemptuous of true religion when it confiscates the taxes of Caesar to finance the things of God.
-*Samuel J. Ervin*

Government is either organized benevolence or organized madness; its peculiar magnitude permits no shading.
-*John Updike*

Government is just a tool, like a hammer. There's nothing intrinsically good or evil about the hammer; it all depends on what it's used for and the skill with which it is used.
-*Molly Ivins*

Government is like a baby. An alimentary canal with a big appetite at one end and no sense of responsibility at the other.
-*Ronald Reagan*

Government is like junior high. Your status depends upon whom you're able to persecute.
-*Jonathan Kellerman*

Government is not reason; it is not eloquence; it is force! Like fire, it is a dangerous servant and a fearful master.
-*George Washington*

Government is the Entertainment division of the military-industrial complex.
-Frank Zappa

Government is the enemy until you need a friend.
-William Cohen

Government is the great fictitious entity by which everyone seeks to live at the expense of everyone else.
-Frederic Bastiat

Government is the only agency which can take a useful commodity like paper, slap some ink on it, and make it totally worthless.
-Ludwig Von Mises

Government is there to do what businesses can't. That's why the Navy doesn't turn a profit.
-Bill Maher

Government is too big and important to be left to the politicians.
-Chester Bowles

Government proposes, bureaucracy disposes. And the bureaucracy must dispose of government proposals by dumping them on us.
-P.J. O'Rourke

Government that breaks its own laws can also easily break you.
-V.S. Naipaul

Government's first duty is to protect the people, not run their lives.
-Ronald Reagan

Government's view of the economy could be summed up in a few short phrases: If it moves, tax it. If it keeps moving, regulate it. And if it stops moving, subsidize it.
-*Ronald Reagan*

Government, the peace-officer at home, breathes war abroad, organizes it into a science, reduces it to a system, makes it a trade, and applauds it as if it were the most honorable work of nations.
-*William Ellery Channing*

Government, today, is growing too strong to be safe. There are no longer any citizens in the world; there are only subjects. They work day in and day out for their masters; they are bound to die for their masters at call. Out of this working and dying they tend to get less and less.
-*H.L. Mencken*

Government, which does not and did not grant us our rights, must not now seek to deny them by using fear as its justification.
-*Malcolm Wallop*

Governments are not built to perceive large truths. Only people can perceive great truths. Governments specialize in small and intermediate truths. They have to be instructed by their people in great truths.
-*Norman Cousins*

Governments do not like to face radical remedies; it is easier to let politics predominate.
-*Barbara Tuchman*

Governments last as long as the undertaxed can defend themselves against the overtaxed.
-*Bernard Berenson*

Governments never learn. Only people learn.
-*Milton Friedman*

Governments want efficient technicians, not human beings, because human beings become dangerous to governments- and to organized religions as well. That is why governments and religious organizations seek to control education.
-*Jiddu Krishnamurti*

Governments, churches, and educational institutes, once the keepers of order and social enlightenment, are now scrambling to remain relevant as our collective consciousness and connectivity grows.
-*George Takei*

Gradually, without noticing it, you turn into a Republican and judge everything on the basis of whether or not it will increase your taxes.
-*Dave Barry*

Grant me thirty years of equal division of inheritances and a free press, and I will provide you with a republic.
-*Alexis de Tocqueville*

Half the American people never read a newspaper. Half never vote for President- the same half?
-*Gore Vidal*

Half the stories in every newspaper should be headlined 'Stop me before I legislate again.'
-*David Boaz*

He always pictured himself a libertarian, which to my way of thinking means 'I want the liberty to grow rich and you can have the liberty to starve.' It's easy to believe that no one should depend on society for help when you yourself happen not to need such help. (on Robert A. Heinlein and libertarian ethics)
-*Isaac Asimov*

He knows nothing; and he thinks he knows everything. That points clearly to a political career.
-*George Bernard Shaw*

He still had a fragment of his boyhood belief that congressmen were persons of intelligence and importance.
-*Sinclair Lewis*

He was born to be a senator. He never said anything important, and he always said it sonorously.
-*Sinclair Lewis*

He was permitted, without restriction, to speak of himself as immoral, agnostic and socialistic, so long as it was universally known that he remained pure, Presbyterian, and Republican.
-*Sinclair Lewis*

He who attacks the fundamentals of the American broadcasting industry attacks democracy itself.
-*William S. Paley*

Hell hath no fury like a liberal scorned.
-*Dick Gregory*

Here in America we are descended in blood and in spirit from revolutionists and rebels- men and women who dare to dissent from accepted doctrine. As their heirs, may we never confuse honest dissent with disloyal subversion.
-*Dwight D. Eisenhower*

Here is my first principle of foreign policy: good government at home.
-*William Gladstone*

Here's the thing about rights. They're not supposed to be voted on. That's why they call them rights.
-*Rachel Maddow*

History suggests that capitalism is a necessary condition for political freedom. Clearly, it is not a sufficient condition.
-*Milton Friedman*

History teaches that wars begin when governments believe the price of aggression is cheap.
-*Ronald Reagan*

History will judge societies and governments- and their institutions- not by how big they are or how well they serve the rich and the powerful, but by how effectively they respond to the needs of the poor and the helpless.
-*Cesar Chavez*

History will record that Jimmy Carter's single contribution to the republic was to fail so completely that he made possible Ronald Reagan's presidency.
-*Thomas Mallon*

Hold on, my friends, to the Constitution of your country and the government established under it. Leave evils which exist in some parts of the country, but which are beyond your control, to the all-wise direction of an over-ruling Providence. Perform those duties which are present, plain and positive. Respect the laws of your country.
-Daniel Webster

Honesty is the best policy; but he who is governed by that maxim is not an honest man.
-Richard Whately

Honor is not the exclusive property of any political party.
-Herbert Hoover

How can a man of integrity get along in Washington?
-Richard P. Feynman

How can you govern a country which has 246 varieties of cheese?
-Charles de Gaulle

How can you look at the Texas legislature and still believe in intelligent design?
-Kinky Friedman

How could you say the best form of government is a republic if you think the universe is a monarchy?
-Alan Watts

How did sex come to be thought of as dirty in the first place? God must have been a Republican.
-Will Durst

How different the new order would be if we could consult the veteran instead of the politician.
-*Henry Miller*

How does it become a man to behave toward this American government today? I answer that he cannot without disgrace be associated with it.
-*Henry David Thoreau*

How little do politics affect the life, the moral life of a nation. One single good book influences the people a vast deal more.
-*William Gladstone*

How prophetic L'Enfant was when he laid it (Washington, DC) out as a city that goes around in circles.
-*John Mason Brown*

How we treat our invalids- our mad, our physically or mentally compromised family members- does tell you something about who we are politically, historically, culturally.
-*Stanley R. Delaney*

Human legislators have, for the most part, chosen to make the sanction of their laws rather vindicatory than remuneratory, or to consist rather in punishments than in actual particular rewards.
-*William Blackstone*

I also wish that the Pledge of Allegiance were directed at the Constitution and the Bill of Rights, as it is when the President takes his oath of office, rather than to the flag and the nation.
-*Carl Sagan*

I always cheer up immensely if an attack is particularly wounding because I think, well, if they attack one personally, it means they have not a single political argument left.
-Margaret Thatcher

I am a Conservative to preserve all that is good in our constitution, a Radical to remove all that is bad. I seek to preserve property and to respect order, and I equally decry the appeal to the passions of the many or the prejudices of the few.
-Benjamin Disraeli

I am a conservative. Quite possibly I am on the losing side; often I think so. Yet, out of a curious perversity I had rather lose with Socrates, let us say, than win with Lenin.
-Russell Kirk

I am amazed that Congressmen can pass a bill imposing severe penalties on anyone who burns the American flag, whereas they are responsible for burning that for which the flag stands.
-Alan Watts

I am an optimist. If I ever quit being an optimist, I guess I'll become a Republican. (as Texas state senator)
-Ray Farabee

I am fed up with a system which busts the pot smoker and lets the big dope racketeer go free.
-George McGovern

I am for free commerce with all nations; political connection with none; and little or no diplomatic establishment.
-George Washington

I am not a member of any organized party- I am a Democrat.
-*Will Rogers*

I am not a politician, and my other habits are good, also.
-*Artemus Ward*

I am not part of the problem. I am a Republican.
-*Dan Quayle (vice president under George H.W. Bush)*

I am obliged to confess I should sooner live in a society governed by the first two thousand names in the Boston telephone directory than in a society governed by the two thousand faculty members of Harvard University.
-*William F. Buckley, Jr.*

I am tired of hearing that democracy doesn't work. Of course it doesn't work. We are supposed to work it.
-*Alexander Woollcott*

I am very suspicious of the activities of governmental agencies.
-*Samuel Gompers*

I asked a man in prison once how he happened to be there and he said he had stolen a pair of shoes. I told him if he had stolen a railroad he would be a United States Senator.
-*Mary Harris Jones (Mother Jones)*

I believe all Southern liberals come from the same starting point- race. Once you figure out they are lying to you about race, you start to question everything.
-*Molly Ivins*

I believe democracy is our greatest export. At least until China figures out a way to stamp it out of plastic for three cents a unit.
-Stephen Colbert

I believe in a wall between church and state so high that no one can climb over it. When religion controls government, political liberty dies; and when government controls religion, religious liberty perishes.
-Samuel J. Ervin

I believe in an America in which the fruits of productivity and prosperity are shared by all, by workers as well as owners, by those at the bottom as well as those at the top; an America in which the sacrifices required by national security are shared by all, by profiteers in the back offices as well as volunteers on the front lines.
-Theodore (Ted) Sorensen

I believe in an America where millions of Americans believe in an America that's the America millions of Americans believe in. That's the America I love. (actual 2012 stump speech)
-Mitt Romney

I believe in the free speech that liberals used to believe in, the economic freedom that conservatives used to believe in, and the personal freedom that America used to believe in.
-Doug Mataconis

I believe that all government is evil, and that trying to improve it is largely a waste of time.
-H.L. Mencken

I believe that all the measures of the Government are directed to the purpose of making the rich richer and the poor poorer.
-William Henry Harrison

I believe that no man who holds a leader's position should ever accept favors from either side. He is then committed to show favors. A leader must stand alone.
-*Mary Harris Jones (Mother Jones)*

I believe that the American concept of civil rights should include not only an observance of our Constitutional Bill of Rights, but also absence of arbitrary action by government in every field.
-*Earl Warren*

I believe that the United States as a government, if it is going to be true to its own founding documents, does have the job of working toward that time when there is no discrimination made on such inconsequential reason as race, color, or religion.
-*Dwight D. Eisenhower*

I believe that the spirit in which American democracy was founded; though often turned aside and often thwarted; can never be defeated or destroyed but that ultimately it will triumph.
-*James Weldon Johnson*

I believe that we are lost here in America, but I believe we shall be found. And this belief, which mounts now to the catharsis of knowledge and conviction, is for me- and I think for all of us- not only our own hope, but America's everlasting, living dream.
-*Thomas Wolfe*

I believe that what separates us all from one another is simply society itself, or, if you like, politics. This is what raises barriers between men, this is what creates misunderstanding.
-*Eugene Ionesco*

The Big Book of American Political Quotations

I believe the most important benefit that I can confer upon my country by my Presidency is to insist upon the entire independence of the executive and legislative branches of the government.
-Grover Cleveland

I believe the preservation of our civil liberties to be the most fundamental and important of all our governmental problems, because it always has been with us and always will be with us and if we ever permit those liberties to be destroyed, there will be nothing left in our system worthy of preservation. They constitute the soul of democracy.
-Earl Warren

I believe there are more instances of the abridgment of the freedom of the people by gradual and silent encroachments of those in power, than by violent and sudden usurpations; but, on a candid examination of history, we shall find that turbulence, violence, and abuse of power, by the majority trampling on the rights of the minority, have produced factions and commotions, which, in republics, have, more frequently than any other cause, produced despotism. If we go over the whole history of ancient and modern republics, we shall find their destruction to have generally resulted from those causes.
-James Madison

I believe there's something out there watching over us. Unfortunately, it's the government.
-Woody Allen

I believe we are on an irreversible trend toward more freedom and democracy- but that could change.
-Dan Quayle (vice president under George H.W. Bush)

I came from a disadvantaged home. They were Republicans.
-Paul Tsongas

I can understand the poor and stupid voting for Marxism or one of its fashionable variants. If you've no hope of being other than a slave, you may as well opt for the most efficient form of slavery.
-*P.D. James*

I can't deny I'm a better ex-president than I was a president.
-*Jimmy Carter*

I contend that the strongest of all governments is that which is most free.
-*William Henry Harrison*

I didn't vote for change, but that's all I have left.
-*Variously attributed*

I dislike Communism because it is undemocratic, and capitalism because it favors exploitation.
-*Bertrand Russell*

I do believe that America's deepest political sickness is that it is a self-righteous nation.
-*Norman Mailer*

I do not despair for our country. I never do. I believe, as I always have, the essential decency and compassion and common sense of the American people will prevail.
-*Jimmy Carter*

I do not know if the people of the United States would vote for superior men if they ran for office, but there can be no doubt that such men do not run.
-*Alexis de Tocqueville*

I do not know which makes a man more conservative- to know nothing but the present, or nothing but the past.
-*John Maynard Keynes*

I do not need to explain why I say things. That's the interesting thing about being the President. Maybe somebody needs to explain to me why they say something, but I don't feel like I owe anybody an explanation. (on *60 Minutes*)
-*George W. Bush*

I do not wish to know what the country does for the rich, they can take care of themselves; but what it does for the poor determines the decency, not to say the civilization, of a government.
-*Frances Willard*

I don't believe in God. My god is patriotism. Teach a man to be a good citizen and you have solved the problem of life.
-*Andrew Carnegie*

I don't believe the Democrats or Republicans are lying to us. I think that every dirty, rotten, lowdown thing they say about each other is true.
-*A. Ray Lambson*

I don't get all choked up about yellow ribbons and American flags. I see them as symbols, and I leave them to the symbol-minded.
-*George Carlin*

I don't have facts on my side... but I still think I'm right. That's the American way.
-*John Green*

The Big Book of American Political Quotations

I don't know a lot about politics, but I can recognize a good party man when I see one.
-*Mae West*

I don't know exactly what democracy is. But we need more of it.
-*(protester, Tianamen Square, 1989)*

I don't know if I can live on my income or not- the government won't let me try it.
-*Bob Thaves*

I don't know much about Americanism, but it's a damn good word with which to carry an election.
-*Warren G. Harding*

I don't know why people think you need government intervention to bring about discrimination; they have no faith in free enterprise.
-*Gordon Fitch*

I don't like the way the Senate has been made a rendezvous for vilification, for selfish political gain at the sacrifice of individual reputations and national unity.
-*Margaret Chase Smith*

I don't measure America by its achievement but by its potential.
-*Shirley Chisholm*

I don't think for a moment that Americans are inherently more stupid or brain-dead than anyone else. It's just that they are routinely provided with conditions that spare them the need to think, so they have got out of the habit.
-*Bill Bryson*

I don't think politics has anything to do with left, right, or center. It has to do with trying to do right by people.
-*Paul Wellstone*

I don't think that a leader can control to any great extent his destiny. Very seldom can he step in and change the situation if the forces of history are running in another direction.
-*Richard M. Nixon*

I don't want to abolish government. I simply want to reduce it to the size where I can drag it into the bathroom and drown it in the bathtub.
-*Grover Norquist*

I don't want to see the Republican Party ride to political victory on the Four Horsemen of Calumny- Fear, Ignorance, Bigotry, and Smear.
-*Margaret Chase Smith*

I fear that the consumer who buys a Confederate flag coffee cup, which she will then put on her American flag place mat, is the sort of sophisticated thinker who is open-minded enough that she is capable of hating blacks and Arabs at the same time.
-*Sarah Vowell*

I grew up in central Illinois midway between Chicago and St. Louis and I made an historic blunder. All my friends became Cardinals fans and grew up happy and liberal and I became a Cubs fan and grew up embittered and conservative.
-*George F. Will*

I hate all bungling as I do sin, but particularly bungling in politics, which leads to the misery and ruin of many thousands and millions of people.
-*Johann Wolfgang von Goethe*

I hate to see them take that creche out of the capitol. It could be the only chance we'll ever have to get three wise men in that building.
-*Ann Richards*

I have always felt that a politician is to be judged by the animosities which he excites among his opponents.
-*Winston Churchill*

I have always found it quaint and rather touching that there is a movement in the US that thinks Americans are not yet selfish enough. (on Libertarians)
-*Christopher Hitchens*

I have been thinking that I would make a proposition to my Republican friends... that if they will stop telling lies about the Democrats, we will stop telling the truth about them.
-*Adlai E. Stevenson II*

I have found that good taste, oddly enough, plays an important role in politics. Why is it like that? The most probable reason is that good taste is a visible manifestation of human sensibility toward the world, environment, people.
-*Vaclav Havel*

I have never found in a long experience of politics that criticism is ever inhibited by ignorance.
-*Harold Macmillan*

I have never had a vote, and I have raised hell all over this country. You don't need a vote to raise hell! You need convictions and a voice!
-*Mary Harris Jones (Mother Jones)*

I have never understood the liberal assumption that if there were justice in the world, there would be fewer rather than more prisoners.
-*Theodore Dalrymple*

I have no use for those- regardless of their political party- who hold some foolish dream of spinning the clock back to days when unorganized labor was a huddled, almost helpless mass.
-*Dwight D. Eisenhower*

I have often thought that the Bill of Rights should have stopped after the first five words: 'Congress shall make no laws...'
-*Variously attributed*

I have terrible short-term memory loss, though I like to think of it as Presidential eligibility.
-*Paula Poundstone*

I have this fear that one day there's going to be a fire in the Senate and there are only going to be 57 Senators there and they'll all die because they won't have the 60 votes to allow themselves to leave the building.
-*Barney Frank*

I have tried to talk about the issues in this campaign... But, strangely enough, my friends, this road has been a lonely road because I never meet anybody coming the other way.
-*Adlai E. Stevenson II*

I have yet to see a piece of writing, political or non-political, that does not have a slant. All writing slants the way a writer leans, and no man is born perpendicular.
-*E.B. White*

The Big Book of American Political Quotations

I hold it, that a little rebellion, now and then, is a good thing, and as necessary in the political world as storms in the physical.
-*Thomas Jefferson*

I hold that democracy cannot be evolved by forcible methods. The spirit of democracy cannot be imposed from without. It has to come from within.
-*Mohandas K. Gandhi*

I hold that public servants are in very truth the servants and not the masters of the people, and that this is true not only of executive and legislative officers but of judicial officers as well.
-*Theodore Roosevelt*

I hope some of the men who get the most votes will be elected.
-*Will Rogers*

I know of no country in which there is so little independence of mind and real freedom of discussion as in America.
-*Alexis de Tocqueville*

I know that when things don't go well they like to blame the Presidents, and that is one of the things which Presidents are paid for.
-*John F. Kennedy*

I like to believe that people in the long run are going to do more to promote peace than our governments. Indeed, I think that people want peace so much that one of these days governments had better get out of the way and let them have it.
-*Dwight D. Eisenhower*

I like to remind people the choice the American electorate had in 1796 for candidates for President. You could choose between the chairman of the American Society of Arts and Letters and the founding president of the American Academy of Sciences. There's been a bit of a decline in the standards of candidacy since then.
-*Christopher Hitchens*

I live in a rather special world. I only know one person who voted for Nixon. Where they are I don't know. They're outside my ken. But sometimes when I'm in a theater I can feel them.
-*Pauline Kael*

I look at politicians as, they are doing what inherently they need to do to retain power. Their job is to consolidate power. When you go to the zoo and you see a monkey throwing poop, you go, 'that's what monkeys do, what are you gonna do?' But what I wish the media would do more frequently is say 'bad monkey.'
-*Jon Stewart*

I look forward to the day when I can be Republican again.
-*John Perry Barlow*

I love a dog, he does nothing for political reasons.
-*Will Rogers*

I love America more than any other country in this world, and, exactly for this reason, I insist on the right to criticize her perpetually.
-*James Baldwin*

I love my government not least for the extent to which it leaves me alone.
-*John Updike*

I make a fortune from criticizing the policy of the government, and then hand it over to the government in taxes to keep it going.
-George Bernard Shaw

I may be president of the United States, but my private life is nobody's damned business.
-Chester A. Arthur

I mean to live my life an obedient man, but obedient to God, subservient to the wisdom of my ancestors; never to the authority of political truths arrived at yesterday at the voting booth.
-William F. Buckley, Jr.

I must follow the people. Am I not their leader?
-Benjamin Disraeli

I must govern the clock, not be governed by it.
-Golda Meir

I must study politics and war that my sons may have liberty to study mathematics and philosophy.
-John Adams

I never had faith that the answers to human problems lay in anything that could be called political. I thought the answers, if there were answers, lay someplace in man's soul.
-Joan Didion

I owed the government $3,400 in taxes. So I sent them two hammers and a toilet seat.
-Sue Murphy

I pay taxes on all the money before it goes into the (Perot Foundation). I think the federal government is a charitable cause, too.
-*H. Ross Perot*

I plead alignment to the flakes of the untitled snakes of a merry cow and to the republicrats for which they scam: one nacho, underpants with licorice and jugs of wine for owls.
-*Matt Groening*

I really believe that in America, if you are clinging to some indefensible, unconstitutional bad idea of a policy, ultimately- one day- you are going to look up from the front gate of your prison and there on the horizon will be the ACLU.
-*Rachel Maddow*

I recognize no moral law in politics. Politics is a game, in which every sort of trick is permissible, and in which the rules are constantly being changed by the players to suit themselves.
-*Adolf Hitler*

I refuse to have an emotional attachment to a piece of ground. At one end of the scale it's called patriotism, at the other end of the scale it's called gardening.
-*Bob Shaw*

I reject the cynical view that politics is inevitably, or even usually, a dirty business.
-*Richard M. Nixon*

I remain just one thing, and one thing only- and that is a clown. It places me on a far higher plane than any politician.
-*Charlie Chaplin*

I said I didn't want to run for president. I didn't ask you to believe me.
-*Mario Cuomo*

I say thank God for government waste. If government is doing bad things, it's only the waste that prevents the harm from being greater.
-*Milton Friedman*

I sit here all day trying to persuade people to do the things they ought to have sense enough to do without my persuading them... that's all the powers of the President amount to.
-*Harry S. Truman*

I still believe in liberalism today as much as I ever did, but, oh, there was a happy time when I believed in liberals...
-*G.K. Chesterton*

I suppose there's a melancholy tone at the back of the American mind, a sense of something lost. And it's the lost world of Thomas Jefferson. It is the lost sense of innocence that we could live with a very minimal state, with a vast sense of space in which to work out freedom.
-*George F. Will*

I tell you folks, all politics is apple sauce.
-*Will Rogers*

I think Democrats made a mistake running away from liberalism. Liberalism- Franklin Roosevelt, Harry Truman, John and Robert Kennedy- that's what the Democratic party ought to reach for.
-*Theodore (Ted) Sorensen*

I think being a liberal, in the true sense, is being non-doctrinaire, non-dogmatic, non-committed to a cause- but examining each case on its merits. Being left of center is another thing; it's a political position. I think most newspapermen by definition have to be liberal; if they're not liberal, by my definition of it, then they can hardly be good newspapermen. If they're preordained dogmatists for a cause, then they can't be very good journalists; that is, if they carry it into their journalism.
-*Walter Cronkite*

I think it is absolutely essential in a democracy to have competition in the media, a lot of competition, and we seem to be moving away from that.
-*Walter Cronkite*

I think it's about time we voted for senators with breasts. After all, we've been voting for boobs long enough.
-*Claire Sargent*

I think it's already apparent that a good part of this Nation understands- if only instinctively- that anything which seems to suggest that God favors a political party or the establishment of a state church, is wrong and dangerous.
-*Mario Cuomo*

I think it's odd that people who cover politics wouldn't have any political views.
-*Nate Silver*

I think politics is an instrument of the devil.
-*Bob Dylan*

I think television has betrayed the meaning of democratic speech, adding visual chaos to the confusion of voices. What role does silence have in all this noise?
-*Frederico Fellini*

I think that Richard Nixon will go down in history as a true folk hero, who struck a vital blow to the whole diseased concept of the revered image and gave the American virtue of irreverence and skepticism back to the people.
-*William S. Burroughs*

I think that you can disagree with people and debate over their positions with issues without engaging in the politics of personal destruction.
-*Hillary Rodham Clinton*

I think that young people who want to understand the world can profit from the works of Plato and Socrates, the behavior of the three Thomases, Aquinas, More and Jefferson- the austere analyses of Immanuel Kant and the political leadership of Abraham Lincoln and Franklin Roosevelt.
-*James A. Michener*

I think the American public wants a solemn ass as a President. And I think I'll go along with them.
-*Calvin Coolidge*

I think the Republican party should be placed in dry dock and have the barnacles scraped off its bottom.
-*Tallulah Bankead*

I think the government solution to a problem is usually as bad as the problem and very often makes the problem worse.
-*Milton Friedman*

I think the most un-American thing you can say is, 'You can't say that.'
-*Garrison Keillor*

I think the right to read is one of our inherent rights, and I think that people in America today are intelligent enough to decide for themselves what they want to read.
-*Bennett Cerf*

I think there are only three things America will be known for 2,000 years from now when they study this civilization: the Constitution, jazz music, and baseball.
-*Gerald Early*

I think we can be reasonably confident that if the American population had the slightest idea of what is being done in their name, they would be utterly appalled.
-*Noam Chomsky*

I try not to tune in to politics until it's two or three months before the election. Till then, it's like watching preseason football.
-*Trey Parker*

I view America like this: 70 to 80 percent (are) pretty reasonable people that truthfully, if they sat down, even on contentious issues, would get along. And the other 20 percent of the country run it.
-*Jon Stewart*

I vote for the same reason that I would punch a bear that was eating me. I don't think it will make a big difference in the outcome, but at least it doesn't look like I want to be eaten by a bear.
-*Nick Doody*

I voted for the Democrats because I didn't like the way the Republicans were running the country. Which is turning out to be like shooting yourself in the head to stop your headache.
-*Jack Mayberry*

I want nothing to do with politicians. Their hearts wither away, and die out of their bodies.
-*Nathaniel Hawthorne*

I was ashamed of being a Republican and afraid of being a Democrat.
-*Robert W. Kenny*

I was born as a Democrat because I was broke. But I started making money... so now I don't know what the hell to do.
-*Marlon Wayans*

I was well on the way to forming my present attitude toward politics as it is practiced in the United States; it is a beautiful fraud that has been imposed on the people for years, whose practitioners exchange gelded promises for the most valuable thing their victims own: their votes. And who benefits the most? The lawyers.
-*Shirley Chisholm*

I will feel equality has arrived when we can elect to office women who are as incompetent as some of the men who are already there.
-*Maureen Reagan*

I wish the government would put a tax on pianos for the incompetent.
-*Edith Sitwell*

I work for a Government I despise for ends I think criminal.
-*John Maynard Keynes*

I worry about my judgment when anything I believe in or do regularly begins to be accepted by the American public.
-George Carlin

I would just warn you that if you get in bed with the government, you'll get more than a good night's sleep.
-Ronald Reagan

I would rather be politically buried than to be hypocritically immortalized.
-Davy Crockett

I wouldn't make the slightest concession for moral leadership. It's much overrated.
-Dean Rusk

I'd accuse the Democrats of being afraid of their own shadow, but I have yet to be convinced they actually cast one.
-Will Durst

I'd be a Libertarian, if they weren't all a bunch of tax-dodging professional whiners.
-Berkeley Breathed

I'd rather vote for something I want and not get it than vote for something I don't want, and get it.
-Eugene V. Debs

I'll be glad to either reply to or dodge your questions, whichever I think will help our election most.
-George Herbert Walker Bush

I'll sign on for results-based pay for teachers the day Congress gets the same deal.
-John Fugelsang

I'm a democrat with a small 'd'.
-George Carlin

I'm a fuzzy-headed warm-hearted liberal, and I think fuzzy-headed warm-hearted liberalism is an ideological stance that needs defending-if necessary, with a hob-nailed boot-kick to the bollocks of budding totalitarianism.
-Charles Stross

I'm a gay Libertarian. I'm one of those 'laisse fairies.'
-Peter McWilliams

I'm a registered Republican and consider socialism a violation of the American principle that you shouldn't stick your nose in other people's business except to make a buck.
-P.J. O'Rourke

I'm a registered Republican, I only seem liberal because I believe that hurricanes are caused by high barometric pressure and not gay marriage. (dialogue from *The Newsroom*)
-Aaron Sorkin

I'm afraid the Constitution doesn't say anything about the separation of church and politics. (dialogue from *The West Wing*)
-Lawrence O'Donnell, Jr.

I'm already suspicious of anyone who thinks he or she is smart enough to be president. You'd have to have some ego to believe that about yourself.
-Andy Rooney

I'm an American who loves an America which doesn't exist, which is a land of freedom and free ideas.
-Bill Hicks

I'm conservative, but I'm not a nut about it.
-George Herbert Walker Bush

I'm fed up to the ears with old men dreaming up wars for young men to die in.
-George McGovern

I'm for democracy, but imposing democracy is an oxymoron. People have to choose democracy, and it has to come up from below.
-Madeleine Albright

I'm not afraid to shake up the system, and government needs more shaking up than any other system I know.
-Ann Richards

I'm not so much interested in politics as I am in overthrowing the government.
-Mort Sahl

I'm really glad that our young people missed the Depression, and missed the great big war. But I do regret that they missed the leaders that I knew. Leaders who told us when things were tough, and that we would have to sacrifice, and these difficulties might last awhile. They didn't tell us things were hard for us because we were different, or isolated, or special interests. They brought us together and they gave us a sense of national purpose.
-Ann Richards

I'm so crazy I plan to vote for Eisenhower again this November.
-Ken Kesey

I'm sorry, but the local news is not the place for government propaganda; it's the place for car chases, kittens caught in trees, and a 'meteorologist' whose previous job was at Hooters.
-*Bill Maher*

I'm sorry, but voting for a presidential candidate because you like the choice for vice president is like getting married to a woman because you like her cat.
-*Kevin G. Barkes*

I've always been a big supporter of the constitutional right of the people to peaceably assemble and petition government for redress of grievances. It's just that I never envisioned it taking the form of thousands of people screaming, 'You asshole, you asshole,' at me.
-*Lowell Weicker*

I've always said that in politics, your enemies can't hurt you, but your friends will kill you.
-*Ann Richards*

I've always felt, in all my books, that there's a deep decency in the American people and a native intelligence- providing they have the facts, providing they have the information.
-*Studs Terkel*

I've been saying for a long time that I'm hoping to find intelligent life in Washington.
-*Arthur C. Clarke*

I've had a tough time learning to act like a congressman. Today I accidentally spent some of my own money.
-*Joseph P. Kennedy II*

I've known personally every president since Jack Kennedy and I can honestly say that Ronald Reagan was the worst. But, he'd have made a hell of a king.
-*Thomas P. (Tip) O'Neill*

Ideas are great arrows, but there has to be a bow. And politics is the bow of idealism.
-*Bill Moyers*

Ideas are inherently conservative. They yield not to the attack of other ideas but to the massive onslaught of circumstance with which they cannot contend.
-*John Kenneth Galbraith*

Ideas matter in American politics, but results matter more.
-*Dan Balz*

If a man is going to be an American at all let him be so without any qualifying adjectives, and if he is going to be something else, let him drop the word American from his personal description.
-*Henry Cabot Lodge*

If all the world's a stage, America is the shiny vertical pole in the middle.
-*John Alejandro King (The Covert Comic)*

If American democracy cannot stand the test of giving to any citizen who measures up to the qualifications required of others the full rights and privileges of American citizenship, then we had just as well abandon that democracy in name as in deed.
-*James Weldon Johnson*

If American politics are too dirty for women to take part in, there's something wrong with American politics.
-*Edna Ferber*

If Congress can do whatever in their discretion can be done by money, and will promote the general welfare, the Government is no longer a limited one possessing enumerated powers, but an indefinite one subject to particular exceptions.
-*James Madison*

If Congress insists on making stupid mistakes and passing foolish tax laws, millionaires should not be condemned if they take advantage of them.
-*J.P. Morgan*

If fascism ever came to the United States, it would be wrapped in an American flag.
-*Huey P. Long*

If God had wanted us to vote, He would have given us candidates.
-*Jay Leno*

If I was a President and wanted something I would claim I didn't want it. Congress has not given any President anything he wanted in the last ten years. Be against anything and then he is sure to get it.
-*Will Rogers*

If she (America) forgets where she came from, if the people lose sight of what brought them along, if she listens to the deniers and mockers, then will begin the rot and dissolution.
-*Carl Sandburg*

If Wall Street paid a tax on every 'game' they run, we would get enough revenue to run the government.
-*Will Rogers*

If a bill is about to pass that really comes down hard on some minority (and) they think it's terribly unfair, it doesn't take much to throw a monkey wrench into this complex system. Americans should appreciate that; they should learn to love the gridlock. It's there so the legislation that does get out is good legislation.
-*Antonin Scalia*

If a conservative is a liberal who's been mugged, a liberal is a conservative who's been arrested.
-*Tom Wolfe*

If a jerk burns the flag, America is not threatened, democracy is not under siege, freedom is not at risk.
-*Gary Ackerman*

If a passion for freedom is not in vogue, patriots may sound the alarm till they are weary.
-*Horace Walpole*

If a political party does not have its foundation in the determination to advance a cause that is right and that is moral, then it is not a political party; it is merely a conspiracy to seize power.
-*Dwight D. Eisenhower*

If a politician found he had cannibals among his constituents, he would promise them missionaries for dinner.
-*H.L. Mencken*

If all power is in the people, if there is no higher law than their will, and if by counting their votes, their will may be ascertained- then the people may entrust all their power to anyone, and the power of the pretender and the usurper is then legitimate. It is not to be challenged since it came originally from the sovereign people.
-*Walter Lippmann*

If an organization carries the word 'united' in its name, it means it isn't, e.g., United Nations, United Arab Republic, United Kingdom, United States.
-*Charles I. Issawi*

If anybody comes up to you and says, 'My kid is a conservative- why is that?' you say, 'Remember in the 60s when we told you if you kept using drugs your kids would be mutants?'
-*Mort Sahl*

If being a liberal means federalizing everything, then I'm no liberal. If being a conservative means turning back the clock; denying problems that exist, then I'm no conservative.
-*Richard M. Nixon*

If dogs talked, one of them would be president by now. Everybody likes dogs.
-*Dean Koontz*

If elected President I'll make sure that dyslexics will have an emergency 119 number. (in a speech to the Alfalfa Club)
-*George W. Bush*

If elected, I will win.
-*Pat Paulsen*

If ever a time should come, when vain and aspiring men shall possess the highest seats in Government, our country will stand in need of its experienced patriots to prevent its ruin.
-*Samuel Adams*

If every nation gets the government it deserves, every generation writes the history which corresponds with its view of the world.
-*Elizabeth Janeway*

If everybody in this town connected with politics had to leave town because of (chasing women) and drinking, you'd have no government.
-*Barry M. Goldwater*

If government were a product, selling it would be illegal.
-*P.J. O'Rourke*

If it is dangerous to suppose that government is always right, it will sooner or later be awkward for public administration if most people suppose that it is always wrong.
-*John Kenneth Galbraith*

If it is true that men are better than women because they are stronger, why aren't our sumo wrestlers in the government?
-*Kishida Toshiko*

If leadership requires a fired-up sense of purpose and imagination, it also demands a profound connection to the society to be led. Like it or not, this is our culture, and we should embrace and celebrate it, even while we strive to refine and shape it.
-*George Takei*

If liberty and equality, as is thought by some, are chiefly to be found in democracy, they will be best attained when all persons alike share in the government to the utmost.
-*Aristotle*

If love is blind, patriotism has lost all five senses.
-*William Blum*

If men will not be governed by the Ten Commandments, they shall be governed by the ten thousand commandments.
-*G.K. Chesterton*

If Moses had spent three years working on the Hill, he would have written the Ten Commandments with three exceptions and a savings clause.
-*Charles Morgan, Jr.*

If one (political) party declared that the earth was flat, the headlines would read 'Views Differ on Shape of Planet.'
-*Paul Krugman*

If one man can be allowed to determine for himself what is law, every man can. That means first chaos, then tyranny. Legal process is an essential part of the democratic process.
-*Felix Frankfurter*

If one morning I walked on top of the water across the Potomac River, the headline that afternoon would read: 'President Can't Swim.'
-*Lyndon B. Johnson*

If our democracy is to flourish, it must have criticism; if our government is to function, it must have dissent.
-*Henry Steele Commager*

If our free society is to endure, and I know it will, those who govern must recognize that the Framers of the Constitution limited their power in order to preserve human dignity and the air of freedom which is our proudest heritage.
-*William J. Brennan, Jr.*

If parties in a republic are necessary to secure a degree of vigilance sufficient to keep the public functionaries within the bounds of law and duty, at that point their usefulness ends. Beyond that they become destructive of public virtue, the parent of a spirit antagonist to that of liberty, and eventually its inevitable conqueror.
-*William Henry Harrison*

If patriotism is 'the last refuge of a scoundrel,' it is not merely because evil deeds may be performed in the name of patriotism.. but because patriotic fervor can obliterate moral distinctions altogether.
-*Ralph Barton Perry*

If people behaved like governments, you'd call the cops.
-*Kelvin Throop, III*

If pigs could vote, the man with the slop bucket would be elected swineherd every time, no matter how much slaughtering he did on the side.
-*Orson Scott Card*

If political authority is not limited, the division of powers, ordinarily the guarantee of freedom, becomes a danger and a scourge.
-*Benjamin Constant*

If politicians and scientists were lazier, how much happier we should all be.
-*Evelyn Waugh*

The Big Book of American Political Quotations

If the American Revolution had produced nothing but the Declaration of Independence, it would have been worthwhile.
-Samuel Eliot Morison

If the Constitution of the United States cannot extend the arm of protection around the weakest and humblest of American citizens as around the strongest and proudest, then it is not worth the paper it is written on.
-James Weldon Johnson

If the Nuremberg laws were applied, then every post-war American president would have been hanged.
-Noam Chomsky

If the average man had had his way there would probably never have been any state. Even today he resents it, classes death with taxes, and yearns for that government which governs least. If he asks for many laws it is only because he is sure that his neighbor needs them; privately he is an unphilosophical anarchist, and thinks laws in his own case superfluous.
-Will Durant

If the presidency is the head of the American body politic, Congress is its gastrointestinal tract. Its vast and convoluted inner workings may be mysterious and unpleasant, but in the end they excrete a great deal of material whose successful passage is crucial to our nation's survival.
-Jon Stewart

If the right to privacy means anything, it is the right of the individual, married or single, to be free from unwarranted government intrusion into matters so fundamentally affecting a person as the decision whether to bear or begat a child.
-William J. Brennan, Jr.

If there are twelve clowns in a ring, you can jump in the middle and start reciting Shakespeare, but to the audience, you'll just be the thirteenth clown. (Walinsky's First Law of Political Campaigns)
-Variously attributed

If there is a bedrock principle of the First Amendment, it is that the government may not prohibit the expression of an idea simply because society finds the idea itself offensive or disagreeable.
-William J. Brennan, Jr.

If there is one eternal truth of politics, it is that there are always a dozen good reasons for doing nothing.
-John le Carré

If they have success, they built it. If they failed, the government ruined it for them. If they get a break, they deserve it. If you get a break, it's a handout and an entitlement. It's a baffling, willfully blind cognitive dissonance.
-Jon Stewart

If voting changed anything, they'd make it illegal.
-Emma Goldman

If we fixed a hangnail the way our government fixes the economy, we'd slam a car door on it.
-Cullen Hightower

If we were directed from Washington when to sow and when to reap, we should all want bread.
-Thomas Jefferson

If you agree with me on 9 out of 12 issues, vote for me. If you agree with me on 12 out of 12 issues, see a psychiatrist.
-Ed Koch

If you ask the government to impose morality, then moral questions will be decided by whoever has the most political power.
-*Harry Browne*

If you begin by saying, 'Thou shalt not lie,' there is no longer any possibility of political action.
-*Jean-Paul Sartre*

If you can find something everyone agrees on, it's wrong.
-*Morris Udall*

If you don't vote, then you may be leaving the decisions up to someone dumber than you.
-*Jesse Ventura*

If you don't vote, you're a moron.
-*Craig Ferguson*

If you don't want a man unhappy politically, don't give him two sides to a question to worry him; give him one. Better yet, give him none.
-*Ray Bradbury*

If you doubt that it is stinky personality that is the driving force behind conservative politics, look back to your pre-political youth. A dollar to a doughnut every one of those childhood friends and acquaintances who was an asshole then is a conservative today.
-*Rack Jite*

If you ever injected truth into politics you have no politics.
-*Will Rogers*

If you go to the city of Washington, you will find that almost all of those corporation lawyers and cowardly politicians, members of Congress, and mis-representatives of the masses claim, in glowing terms, that they have risen from the ranks to places of eminence and distinction. I am very glad that I cannot make that claim for myself. I would be ashamed to admit that I had risen from the ranks. When I rise it will be with the ranks, and not from the ranks.
-*Eugene V. Debs*

If you have a weak candidate and a weak platform, wrap yourself up in the American flag and talk about the Constitution.
-*Matthew Stanley Quay*

If you look at how the federal government spends our money, it's an insurance conglomerate protected by a large, standing army.
-*Ezra Klein*

If you maintain a consistent political position long enough, you will eventually be accused of treason.
-*Mort Sahl*

If you make less than $50,000 a year and vote Republican, you are a moron.
-*Rack Jite*

If you put the federal government in charge of the Sahara Desert, in five years there'd be a shortage of sand.
-*Milton Friedman*

If you think too much about being re-elected, it is very difficult to be worth re-electing.
-*Woodrow Wilson*

If you voted for change, you better start counting it.
-*Variously attributed*

If you want government to intervene domestically, you're a liberal. If you want government to intervene overseas, you're a conservative. If you want government to intervene everywhere, you're a moderate. If you don't want government to intervene anywhere, you're an extremist.
-*Joseph Sobran*

If you want to study the social and political history of modern nations, study hell.
-*Thomas Merton*

If you're listening to a rock star in order to get your information on who to vote for, you're a bigger moron than they are. Why are we rock stars? Because we're morons.
-*Alice Cooper*

If you're sick and tired of the politics of cynicism and polls and principles, come and join this campaign.
-*George W. Bush*

If your success is defined as being well adjusted to injustice and well adapted to indifference then we don't want successful leaders. We want great leaders- who love the people enough and respect the people enough to be unsought, unbound, unafraid and unintimidated to tell the truth.
-*Cornel West*

In 1929 the wise, far-seeing electors of my native Hereford sent me to Westminster and, two years later, the lousy bastards kicked me out.
-*Frank Owen*

In 1960, when I came out of prison as an ex-convict, I had more freedom under parolee supervision than there's available... in America right now.
-Merle Haggard

In a way, J.F.K. was the high point of the American dream. In order to go to the moon and back, all we did was say we could- and we did.
-Richard Dreyfuss

In America any boy may become President, and I suppose it's just one of the risks he takes.
-Adlai E. Stevenson II

In America everybody is of the opinion that he has no social superiors, since all men are equal, but he does not admit that he has no social inferiors, for, from the time of Jefferson onward, the doctrine that all men are equal applies only upwards, not downwards.
-Bertrand Russell

In America the absence of honest passion is a distinguishing feature of both professional wrestling and politics.
-Murray Kempton

In America we can say what we think, and even if we can't think, we can say it anyhow
-Charles F. Kettering

In America we have no kings. We have front runners.
-Howard Fineman

In America you can say anything you want- as long as it doesn't have any effect.
-Paul Goodman

In America, an acquittal doesn't mean you're innocent, it means you beat the rap. My clients lose even when they win.
-F. Lee Bailey

In America, even a poor boy can grow up to win the support of powerful special interest groups.
-John Callahan

In America, health is not regarded as a right, but as a commodity to be bought and sold just like anything else. There are places where an ambulance team will investigate your financial health before it will have any truck with your physical health.
-William Golding

In America, through pressure of conformity, there is freedom of choice, but nothing to choose from.
-Peter Ustinov

In Dr. Johnson's famous dictionary patriotism is defined as the last resort of a scoundrel. Will all due respect to an enlightened but inferior lexicographer I beg to submit that it is the first.
-Ambrose Bierce

In a body (like Congress) where there are more than one hundred talking lawyers, you can make no calculation upon the termination of any debate.
-Franklin P. Adams

In a country well governed, poverty is something to be ashamed of. In a country badly governed, wealth is something to be ashamed of.
-Confucius

In a democracy dissent is an act of faith. Like medicine, the test of its value is not in its taste, but in its effects.
-Senator J. William Fulbright

In a democracy the people choose a leader in whom they trust. Then the chosen leader says, 'Now shut up and obey me.' People and party are then no longer free to interfere in his business.
-Max Weber

In a democracy, a man who does not listen cannot lead.
-David Broder

In a democracy, the votes of the vicious and stupid count. On the other hand, in any other system, they might be running the show.
-Variously attributed

In a democracy, you don't look up to people, you look sideways at your fellow citizens.
-Robert Hughes

In a democracy, you say what you like and do what you're told.
-Dave Barry

In a democratic age, only the behavior of the authorities is subject to public criticism; that of the people themselves, never.
-Theodore Dalrymple

In a democratic society like ours, relief must come through an aroused popular conscience that sears the conscience of the people's representatives.
-Felix Frankfurter

In a democratic society, you're supposed to be an activist; that is, you participate. It could be a letter written to an editor.
-Studs Terkel

In a free society a large degree of human activity is none of the government's business. We should make criminal what's going to hurt other people and other than that we should leave it to people to make their own choices.
-Barney Frank

In a government of laws, existence of the government will be imperiled if it fails to observe the law scrupulously.
-Louis Brandeis

In a political fight, when you've got nothing in favor of your side, start a row in the opposition camp.
-Huey P. Long

In a political struggle, never get personal else the dagger digs too deep. Your enemy today may need to be your ally tomorrow.
-Jack Valenti

In a rational society we would want our presidents to be teachers. In our actual society we insist they be cheerleaders.
-Steve Allen

In addition, as citizens, we must fight in their incipient stages all movements by government or party or pressure groups that seek to limit the legitimate liberties of any of our fellow citizens.
-Wendell Willkie

In all history there is no war which was not hatched by the governments, the governments alone, independent of the interests of the people, to whom war is always pernicious even when successful.
-*Leo Tolstoy*

In all matters of government the correct answer is usually: Do nothing.
-*Robert A. Heinlein*

In any relatively close election you can generally credit almost any subgroup as providing the marginal votes.
-*Duncan Black*

In democracy it's your vote that counts. In feudalism it's your count that votes.
-*Mogens Jallberg*

In democratic society each citizen is habitually busy with the contemplation of a very petty object, which is himself.
-*Alexis de Tocqueville*

In every political society, parties are unavoidable. A difference of interests, real or supposed, is the most natural and fruitful source of them. The great object should be to combat the evil: 1. By establishing a political equality among all. 2. By withholding unnecessary opportunities from a few, to increase the inequality of property, by an immoderate, and especially an unmerited, accumulation of riches. 3. By the silent operation of laws, which, without violating the rights of property, reduce extreme wealth towards a state of mediocrity, and raise extreme indigence towards a state of comfort. 4. By abstaining from measures which operate differently on different interests, and particularly such as favor one interest at the expence of another. 5. By making one party a check on the other, so far as the existence of parties cannot be prevented, nor their views accommodated. If this is not the language of reason, it is that of republicanism.
-*James Madison*

In every well governed state, wealth is a sacred thing; in democracies it is the only sacred thing.
-*Anatole France*

In framing a government which is to be administered by men over men, the great difficulty lies in this: you must first enable the government to control the governed; and in the next place oblige it to control itself.
-*James Madison*

In government offices which are sensitive to the vehemence and passion of mass sentiment public men have no sure tenure. They are in effect perpetual office seekers, always on trial for their political lives, always required to court their restless constituents.
-*Walter Lippmann*

In government the sin of pride manifests itself in the recurring delusion that things are under control.
-George F. Will

In government, the scum rises to the top.
-Friedrich Hayek

In life, it is never the big battle, the big moment, the big speech, the big election. That does not change things. What changes things is every day, getting up and rendering small acts of service and love beyond that what's expected of you or required of you.
-Cory Booker

In making the great experiment of governing people by consent rather than by coercion, it is not sufficient that the party in power should have a majority. It is just as necessary that the party in power should never outrage the minority.
-Walter Lippmann

In modern America, anyone who attempts to write satirically about the events of the day finds it difficult to concoct a situation so bizarre that it may not actually come to pass while the article is still on the presses.
-Calvin Trillin

In monarchy the crime of treason may admit of being pardoned or lightly punished, but the man who dares rebel against the laws of a republic ought to suffer death.
-Samuel Adams

In most places in the country, voting is looked upon as a right and a duty, but in Chicago it's a sport.
-Dick Gregory

The Big Book of American Political Quotations

In most poetic expressions of patriotism, it is impossible to distinguish what is one of the greatest human virtues from the worst human vice, collective egotism.
-W.H. Auden

In my lifetime, we've gone from Eisenhower to George W. Bush. We've gone from John F. Kennedy to Al Gore. If this is evolution, I believe that in twelve years, we'll be voting for plants.
-Lewis Black

In nature, stupidity gets you killed. In the workplace, it gets you fired. In politics, it gets you re-elected.
-Bill VanRemmen

In order to become the master, the politician poses as the servant.
-Charles de Gaulle

In order to rally people, governments need enemies. They want us to be afraid, to hate, so we will rally behind them. And if they do not have a real enemy, they will invent one in order to mobilize us.
-Thich Nhat Hanh

In our brief national history we have shot four of our presidents, worried five of them to death, impeached one and hounded another out of office. And when all else fails, we hold an election and assassinate their character.
-P.J. O'Rourke

In our system, at about 11:30 on election night, they just push you off the edge of the cliff and that's it. You might scream on the way down, but you're going to hit the bottom, and you're not going to be in elective office.
-Walter Mondale

In our time, political speech and writing are largely the defense of the indefensible.
-*George Orwell*

In political combat, as in speed contests among horses, the outcome becomes doubtful only after the entry of the second contestant.
-*Warren Burnett*

In political institutions, almost everything we call an abuse was once a remedy.
-*Joseph Joubert*

In political matters it is very hard for a man in office to be purer than his neighbors- and, when he is so, he becomes troublesome.
-*Anthony Trollope*

In politics it is necessary either to betray one's country or the electorate. I prefer to betray the electorate.
-*Charles de Gaulle*

In politics nothing is immutable. Events carry within them an invincible power. The unwise destroy themselves in resistance. The skillful accept events, take strong hold of them and direct them.
-*Napoleon Bonaparte*

In politics people build whole reputations off of getting one thing right.
-*Nate Silver*

In politics the middle way is none at all.
-*John Adams*

In politics you can't be true to all of your friends all of the time.
-*Perry S. Heath*

In politics you have no friends, only allies.
-*John F. Kennedy*

In politics you must always keep running with the pack. The moment that you falter and they sense that you are injured, the rest will turn on you like wolves.
-*R.A. Butler*

In politics, a community of hatred is almost always the foundation of friendship.
-*Alexis de Tocqueville*

In politics, a lie unanswered becomes truth within 24 hours.
-*San Francisco Mayor Willie L. Brown, Jr.*

In politics, an absurdity is not an impediment.
-*Napoleon Bonaparte*

In politics, as in religion, it is equally absurd to aim at making proselytes by fire and sword. Heresies in either can rarely be cured by persecution.
-*Alexander Hamilton*

In politics, if you want anything said, ask a man. If you want anything done, ask a woman.
-*Margaret Thatcher*

In politics, it seems, retreat is honorable if dictated by military considerations and shameful if even suggested for ethical reasons.
-*Mary McCarthy*

In politics, merit is rewarded by the possessor being raised, like a target, to a position to be fired at.
-*Christian Bovee*

In politics, nothing is contemptible.
-*Benjamin Disraeli*

In politics, nothing is permanent and, therefore, nothing is too late.
-*Bill Clinton*

In politics, the things that do not happen are frequently as significant as those that do.
-*Theodore H. White*

In politics, what begins in fear usually ends in folly.
-*Samuel Taylor Coleridge*

In reality it is far less prejudicial to witness the immorality of the great than to witness that immorality which leads to greatness.
-*Alexis de Tocqueville*

In really hard times the rules of the game are altered. The inchoate mass begins to stir. It becomes potent, and when it strikes... it strikes with incredible emphasis. Those are the rare occasions when a national will emerges from the scattered, specialized, or indifferent blocs of voters who ordinarily elect the politicians. Those are for good or evil the great occasions in a nation's history.
-*Walter Lippmann*

In rivers and bad governments, the lightest things swim at the top.
-*Benjamin Franklin*

In the case of the American presidency it is the machine which drives the driver, and the driver is only required to make reassuring gestures of being in charge of the machine.
-*Peter Ustinov*

In the First Amendment the Founding Fathers gave the free press the protection it must have to fulfill its essential role in our democracy. The press was to serve the governed, not the governors. The Government's power to censor the press was abolished so that the press would remain forever free to censure the Government. The press was protected so that it could bare the secrets of government and inform the people. Only a free and unrestrained press can effectively expose deception in government.
-Hugo Black

In the US the people are blinkered by the millions of flags that flutter on the forest of poles and hang from every other window. They block the political view and the thunder of their flapping means that even anxious questions, let alone protests, cannot, will not, be heard.
-Phillip Adams

In the United States, anybody can be president. That's the problem.
-George Carlin

In the United States, doing good has come to be, like patriotism, a favorite device of persons with something to sell.
-H.L. Mencken

In the United States, politics is a profession, whereas in Europe it is a right and a duty.
-Umberto Eco

In the councils of government, we must guard against the acquisition of unwarranted influence, whether sought or unsought, by the military-industrial complex. The potential for the disastrous rise of misplaced power exists and will persist. We must never let the weight of this combination endanger our liberties or democratic processes. We should take nothing for granted. Only an alert and knowledgeable citizenry can compel the proper meshing of the huge industrial and military machinery of defense with our peaceful methods and goals, so that security and liberty may prosper together.
-Dwight D. Eisenhower

In the democratic western countries so-called capitalism leads a saturnalia of 'freedom,' like a bastard brother of reform.
-Wyndham Lewis

In the digital age our idea of political activism is forwarding an e-mail. You copy four people and think, 'I've effin' done my part for today.'
-Marc Maron

In the future, most democratic countries will be led by tall people with good hair.
-Scott Adams

In the great fulfillment we must have a citizenship less concerned about what the government can do for it and more anxious about what it can do for the nation.
-Warren G. Harding

In the last analysis, politics is not predictions and politics is not observations. Politics is what we do. Politics is what we do, politics is what we create, by what we work for, by what we hope for and what we dare to imagine.
-Paul Wellstone

In the legislature, promptitude of decision is oftener an evil than a benefit.
-*Alexander Hamilton*

In the lexicon of the political class, the word 'sacrifice' means that the citizens are supposed to mail even more of their income to Washington so that the political class will not have to sacrifice the pleasure of spending it.
-*George F. Will*

In the world at large, we cannot lead if our leaders mislead.
-*Jimmy Carter*

In this era of the global village, the tide of democracy is running. And it will not cease, not in China, not in South Africa, not in any corner of this earth, where the simple idea of democracy and freedom has taken root.
-*Paul Tsongas*

In this country American means white. Everybody else has to hyphenate.
-*Toni Morrison*

In this possibly terminal phase of human existence, democracy and freedom are more than just ideals to be valued- they may be essential to survival.
-*Noam Chomsky*

In this world of sin and sorrow there is always something to be thankful for; as for me, I rejoice that I am not a Republican.
-*H.L. Mencken*

In time of war the loudest patriots are the greatest profiteers.
-*August Bebel*

In view of the tide of religiosity engulfing a once secular republic it is refreshing to be reminded by Freethinkers that free thought and skepticism are robustly in the American tradition. After all the Founding Fathers began by omitting God from the American Constitution.
-*Arthur Schlesinger, Jr.*

In your country club, your church and business, about 15 percent of the people are screwballs, lightweights and boobs and you would not want those people unrepresented in Congress.
-*Alan Simpson*

Indeed, the ideal for a well-functioning democratic state is like the ideal for a gentleman's well-cut suit- it is not noticed. For the common people of Britain, Gestapo and concentration camps have approximately the same degree of reality as the monster of Loch Ness. Atrocity propaganda is helpless against this healthy lack of imagination.
-*Arthur Koestler*

Individual rights are not subject to a public vote; a majority has no right to vote away the rights of a minority; the political function of rights is precisely to protect minorities from oppression by majorities.
-*Ayn Rand*

Individuality is the aim of political liberty. By leaving the citizen as much freedom of action and of being as comports with order and the rights of others, the institutions render him truly a freeman. He is left to pursue his means of happiness in his own manner.
-*James Fenimore Cooper*

Information is the currency of democracy.
-*Thomas Jefferson*

Innocents are the least successful presidents.
-*Steven J. Rubenzer*

Instant analysis is the occupational disease. There are no smoke-stacks, there's no black lung. Politics is the only industry.
-*Kirk O'Donnell*

Instead of giving a politician the keys to the city, it might be better to change the locks.
-*Doug Larson*

Institutions may crumble and governments fall, but it is only that they may renew a better youth, and mount upwards like the eagle.
-*George Bancroft*

Institutions purely democratic must, sooner, or later, destroy liberty or civilization or both.
-*Thomas Babington Macaulay*

Invest in America. Buy a Congressman. (T-shirt)
-*Variously attributed*

Is there really someone who, searching for a group of wise and sensitive persons to regulate him for his own good, would choose that group of people that constitute the membership of both houses of Congress?
-*Robert Nozick*

It does no harm just once in a while to acknowledge that the whole country isn't in flames, that there are people in the country besides politicians, entertainers, and criminals.
-*Charles Kuralt*

It doesn't matter who you vote for, the government always gets in.
-Variously attributed

It feels like all the people who want limited government really just want government limited to Republicans.
-Jon Stewart

It has become more and more obvious that there is one political party in America, and that is The Business Party.
-Bill Hicks

It has been the great fault of our politicians that they have all wanted to do something.
-Anthony Trollope

It has too often been too easy for rulers and governments to incite man to war.
-Lester B. Pearson

It is a besetting vice of democracies to substitute public opinion for law. This is the usual form in which masses of men exhibit their tyranny.
-James Fenimore Cooper

It is a function of government to invent philosophies to explain the demands of its own convenience.
-Murray Kempton

It is a governing principle of nature, that the agency which can produce most good, when perverted from its proper aim, is most productive of evil.
-James Fenimore Cooper

It is a great advantage to a President and a major source of safety to the country, for him to know he is not a great man.
-*Calvin Coolidge*

It is a politician's business to get and hold his job at all costs. It is seldom a mistake.
-*H.L. Mencken*

It is a strange fact that freedom and equality, the two basic ideas of democracy, are to some extent contradictory. Logically considered, freedom and equality are mutually exclusive, just as society and the individual are mutually exclusive.
-*Thomas Mann*

It is absolutely vital for every American to watch CNN for five minutes a day. Why? Because it'll give you a good idea of what it's gonna be like when you have a stroke.
-*Lewis Black*

It is an obvious and blatant stupidity beyond my ability to articulate how dumb it is for us not to teach our children how to run the government.
-*Richard Dreyfuss*

It is astonishing with how little wisdom mankind can be governed, when that little wisdom is its own.
-*William R. Inge*

It is better to vote for what you want and not get it than to vote for what you don't want and get it.
-*Eugene V. Debs*

It is contended by many that ours is a Christian government, founded upon the Bible, and that all who look upon the book as false or foolish are destroying the foundation of our country. The truth is, our government is not founded upon the rights of gods, but upon the rights of men. Our Constitution was framed, not to declare and uphold the deity of Christ, but the sacredness of humanity. Ours is the first government made by the people and for the people. It is the only nation with which the gods have had nothing to do. And yet there are some judges dishonest and cowardly enough to solemnly decide that this is a Christian country, and that our free institutions are based upon the infamous laws of Jehovah.
-Robert G. Ingersoll

It is dangerous to be right when the government is wrong.
-Voltaire (François Marie Arouet)

It is difficult for a statesman who still has a political future to reveal everything that he knows.
-George Orwell

It is error alone which needs the support of government. Truth can stand by itself.
-Thomas Jefferson

It is from weakness that people reach for dictators and concentrated government power. Only the strong can be free. And only the productive can be strong.
-Wendell Willkie

It is futile to try and win democracy abroad, while we are losing it at home. (in a letter to President Woodrow Wilson)
-Upton Sinclair

It is hard for anyone to be an honest politician who is not born and bred a Dissenter.
-William Hazlitt

It is horrifying that we have to fight our own Government to save the environment.
-Ansel Adams

It is important that the United States remain a two-party system. I'm a fellow who likes small parties and the Republican Party can't be too small to suit me.
-Lyndon B. Johnson

It is ironic that the United States should have been founded by intellectuals, for throughout most of our political history, the intellectual has been for the most part either an outsider, a servant or a scapegoat.
-Richard Hofstadter

It is ironic to think of the number of people in this country who pray for the poor and needy on Sunday and spend the rest of the week complaining that the government is doing something about them.
-William Sloane Coffin, Jr.

It is just as impossible to help reform by conciliating prejudice as it is by buying votes. Prejudice is the enemy. Whoever is not for you is against you.
-John Jay Chapman

It is known, however, that men enter local politics solely as a result of being unhappily married.
-C. Northcote Parkinson

It is lamentable that to be a good patriot, one must become an enemy of the rest of mankind.
-*Voltaire (François Marie Arouet)*

It is my experience that most claims of national security are part of a campaign to avoid telling the truth.
-*Ben Bradlee*

It is my experience that the best way to deal with American politics is 50 milligrams of Zoloft three times a day.
-*Will Durst*

It is not by the consolidation, or concentration, of powers, but by their distribution that good government is effected.
-*Thomas Jefferson*

It is not impossible to govern Italians. It is merely useless.
-*Benito Mussolini*

It is not in the nature of politics that the best men should be elected. The best men do not want to govern their fellowmen.
-*George MacDonald*

It is not the function of our government to keep the citizen from falling into error; it is the function of the citizen to keep the government from falling into error.
-*Robert H. Jackson*

It is not the reporter's job to be a patriot or to presume to determine where patriotism lies. His job is to relate the facts.
-*Walter Cronkite*

It is of the utmost danger to society to make it (religion) a party in political disputes.
-*Thomas Paine*

It is only the present danger of immediate evil or an intent to bring it about that warrants Congress in setting a limit to the expression of opinion where private rights are not concerned.
-*Oliver Wendell Holmes, Jr.*

It is our experience that political leaders do not always mean the opposite of what they say.
-*Abba Eban*

It is part of the American character to consider nothing desperate.
-*Thomas Jefferson*

It is poor government that does not realize that the prolonged life, health and happiness of its people are its greatest asset.
-*William James Mayo*

It is possible that the distinction between moral relativism and moral absolutism has sometimes been blurred because an excessively consistent practice of either leads to the same practical result- ruthlessness in political life.
-*Richard Hofstadter*

It is possible to read the history of this country as one long struggle to extend the liberties established in our Constitution to everyone in America.
-*Molly Ivins*

It is preposterous to suppose that the people of one generation can lay down the best and only rules of government for all who are to come after them, and under unforeseen contingencies.
-*Ulysses S. Grant*

It is rare that a legislature reasons. It is too quickly impassioned.
-*Napoleon Bonaparte*

It is simply untrue that all our institutions are evil... that all politicians are mere opportunists, that all aspects of university life are corrupt. Having discovered an illness, it's not terribly useful to prescribe death as a cure.
-*George McGovern*

It is the belief that extremes and excesses of inequality must be reduced so that each person is free to fully develop his or her full potential. This is why we take precious time out of our lives and give it to politics.
-*Paul Wellstone*

It is the duty of a patriot to protect his country from its government.
-*Thomas Paine*

It is the duty of government to make it difficult for people to do wrong, easy to do right.
-*William Gladstone*

It is the media that controls the boundaries of what is politically permissible, so better to change the media.
-*Julian Assange*

It is the patriotic duty of every man to lie for his country.
-*Alfred Adler*

It is time to dismantle government secrecy, this most pervasive of Cold War-era regulations. It is time to begin building the supports for the era of openness that is already upon us.
-Daniel Patrick Moynihan

It is true that many Americans find the (Ten) Commandments in accord with their personal beliefs. But we do not count heads before enforcing the First Amendment.
-Sandra Day O'Connor

It is very comforting to believe that leaders who do terrible things are, in fact, mad. That way, all we have to do is make sure we don't put psychotics in high places and we've got the problem solved.
-Tom Wolfe

It is, therefore, a just political maxim, that every man must be supposed a knave: Though at the same time, it appears somewhat strange, that a maxim should be true in politics, which is false in fact.
-David Hume

It makes no difference who you vote for- the two parties are really one party representing four percent of the people.
-Gore Vidal

It may be laid as a universal rule that a government which attempts more than it ought will perform less.
-Thomas Babington Macaulay

It may make your blood boil and your mind may not be changed, but the practice of listening to opposing views is essential for effective citizenship. It is essential for our democracy.
-Barack Obama

It only takes 20 years for a liberal to become a conservative without changing a single idea.
-Robert Anton Wilson

It seems to be the profession of a President simply to hear other people talk.
-William Howard Taft

It seems to be true, particularly in middle America, that those most militant about using up fossil fuels, don't actually believe in fossils.
-Ricky Gervais

It should be mandatory that every president would read the Constitution. Too many swear to uphold the Constitution and then make end runs around it.
-Helen Thomas

It takes a village to raise a child. The village is Washington. You are the child.
-P.J. O'Rourke

It takes nerve to be a Democrat, but it takes money to be a Republican.
-Will Rogers

It used to be that we disagreed over the basic facts we were fighting over, and we had different opinions about them. Now I think we accept different sources of authority.
-Rachel Maddow

It was just so in the American Revolution, in 1776, the first delicacy the men threw overboard in Boston harbor was the tea, woman's favorite beverage. The tobacco and whiskey, though heavily taxed, they clung to with the tenacity of the devil-fish.
-Elizabeth Cady Stanton

It will be impossible to establish a higher political life than the people themselves crave.
-Jane Addams

It's a great country, where anybody can grow up to be president... except me.
-Barry M. Goldwater

It's a great day for America, everybody!
-Craig Ferguson

It's a moral problem that the government is making into criminals people, who may be doing something you and I don't approve of, but who are doing something that hurts nobody else.
-Milton Friedman

It's about time that we create first class citizenship for every American plain and simple. Every New Jersey-ian. This should not be a popular vote. This is something we should do now.
-Cory Booker

It's almost impossible to be funnier than the people in Washington.
-Carol Burnett

It's better to have died a small child than to be a politician who gets caught in a scandal during a slow news month.
-Lewis Grizzard

It's every American's duty to support his government, but not necessarily in the style to which it has become accustomed.
-Thomas Clifford

It's getting harder and harder to tell government from show business.
-Michael J. Rosen

It's hard to argue with the government. Remember, they run the Bureau of Alcohol, Tobacco and Firearms, so they must know a thing or two about satisfying women.
-Scott Adams

It's harder to be a Liberal than a Conservative because it is easier to give someone the finger than a helping hand.
-Mike Royko

It's kind of ironic. The only time you can be really be sure that a politician is telling the truth is when he's admitting that he's a crook.
-Jay Leno

It's like, duh. Just when you thought there wasn't a dime's worth of difference between the two parties, the Republicans go and prove you're wrong.
-Molly Ivins

It's not the voting that's democracy; it's the counting.
-Tom Stoppard

It's safe to assume that by 2085 guns will be sold in vending machines but you won't be able to smoke anywhere in America.
-David Sedaris

It's quite possible to do anything, but not to put it on the leaders and the parking meters. Don't expect Jimmy Carter or Ronald Reagan or John Lennon or Yoko Ono or Bob Dylan or Jesus Christ to come and do it for you. You have to do it yourself.
-*John Lennon*

It's very hard to stand up to the government which is saying that publication will threaten national security. People don't seem to realize that reporters and editors know something about national security and care deeply about it.
-*Ben Bradlee*

Jesus was a first-century Jew, and when we try to make him into a twenty-first century American we distort everything he was and everything he stood for.
-*Bart D. Ehrman*

Jesus would not be crucified today. The prophets would not be stoned. Socrates would not drink the hemlock. They would instead be banned from the Sunday talk shows and op-ed pages by the sentries of establishment thinking who guard against dissent with the one weapon of mass destruction most cleverly designed to obliterate democracy: the rubber stamp.
-*Bill Moyers*

Journalism is one of the devices whereby industrial autocracy keeps its control over political democracy; it is the day-by-day, between-elections propaganda, whereby the minds of the people are kept in a state of acquiescence, so that when the crisis of an election comes, they go to the polls and cast their ballots for either one of the two candidates of their exploiters.
-*Upton Sinclair*

Just about the time you finally see light at the end of the tunnel, you find out it's a Government Project to build more tunnel.
-*Variously attributed*

Just as it would be madness to settle on medical treatment for the body of a person by taking an opinion poll of the neighbors, so it is irrational to prescribe for the body politic by polling the opinions of the people at large.
-*Plato*

Just because you do not take an interest in politics doesn't mean politics won't take an interest in you.
-*Pericles*

Justice is the end of Government. It is the end of civil society. It ever has been, and ever will be pursued, until it be obtained, or until liberty be lost in the pursuit.
-*James Madison*

Justices look solemn in their formal black robes, but every so often they like to have a little fun by taking on a strange case, or overturning a presidential election, that sort of thing.
-*Christopher Buckley*

Labor Day is a great American holiday that people celebrate by going out and buying products made in China.
-*David Letterman*

Laughter is America's most important export.
-*Walt Disney*

Leadership consists of nothing but taking responsibility for everything that goes wrong and giving your subordinates credit for everything that goes well.
-Dwight D. Eisenhower

Leadership is a potent combination of strategy and character. But if you must be without one, be without the strategy.
-H. Norman Schwartzkopf, Jr.

Leadership is more likely to be assumed by the aggressive than by the able, and those who scramble to the top are more often motivated by their own inner torments.
-Bergen Evans

Leadership is not a position or a title, it is action and example.
-Cory Booker

Leadership is the art of getting someone else to do something you want done because he wants to do it.
-Dwight D. Eisenhower

Leadership is, among other things, the ability to inflict pain and get away with it- short-term pain for long-term gain.
-George F. Will

Legislation is a matter of more or less intelligent improvisation aiming at palliating conditions by means of patchwork policies.
-John Dewey

Legislators and revolutionaries who promise equality and liberty at the same time are either psychopaths or mountebanks.
-Johann Wolfgang von Goethe

Legislators represent people, not trees or acres. Legislators are elected by voters, not farms or cities or economic interests.
-Earl Warren

Legislators who are of even average intelligence stand out among their colleagues.
-Bergen Evans

Legislators: Rape their wives and do two years. Kill their children and do five years. Steal their money and kiss your ass goodbye.
-L.R. Powell

Let me tell you, sisters, seeing dried egg on a plate in the morning is a lot dirtier than anything I've had to deal with in politics.
-Ann Richards

Let the people think they govern and they will be governed.
-William Penn

Let us wage a moral and political war against the billionaires and corporate leaders, on Wall Street and elsewhere, whose policies and greed are destroying the middle class of America.
-Bernie Sanders

Let's give some substance to patriotism. It may take a generation.
-Richard Dreyfuss

Let's not be too rough on our own ignorance; it's what makes America great!
-Frank Zappa

Liberal comes from the Latin liberalis, which means pertaining to a free man. In politics, to be liberal is to want to extend democracy through change and reform. One can see why the word had to be erased from our political lexicon.
-Gore Vidal

Liberal is just another way of saying 'prematurely mainstream.'
-John Fugelsang

Liberal learning is both a safeguard against false ideas of freedom and a source of true ones.
-Alfred Whitney Griswold

Liberalism is the philosophy for our time, because it does not try to conserve every tradition of the past, because it does not apply to new problems the old doctrinaire solutions, because it is prepared to experiment and innovate and because it knows that the past is less important than the future.
-Pierre Elliott Trudeau

Liberalism is the right to question without being called a heretic. That's what America did for the world.
-Jack Nicholson

Liberalism is trust of the people tempered by prudence; conservativism is distrust of the people tempered by fear.
-William Gladstone

Liberalism regards all absolutes with profound skepticism, including both moral imperatives and final solutions... Insistence upon any particular solution is the mark of an ideologue...
-Arthur Schlesinger, Jr.

Liberalism, above all, means emancipation- emancipation from one's fears, his inadequacies, from prejudice, from discrimination... from poverty.
-Hubert H. Humphrey

Liberalism: for every complicated problem there exists both an intellectual and a moral solution and they coincide.
-Theodore H. White

Liberals claim to want to give a hearing to other views, but then are shocked and offended to discover that there are other views.
-William F. Buckley, Jr.

Liberals feel unworthy of their possessions. Conservatives feel they deserve everything they've stolen.
-Mort Sahl

Libertarian is the Latin term for 'Embarrassed Republican.'
-John Fugelsang

Libertarianism fails for me, not because I don't value freedom, but because it exalts ideology over practicality, just as its communist and anarchist cousins do.
-Kevin Brennan

Libertarianism only exists to give young Republicans something marginally less repulsive to call themselves when they're trying to get laid.
-Roy Edroso

Libertarians are conservatives who still get high.
-Drew Carey

Libertarians are not the brightest lights in the candelabra, a fact that is evident from the alternatives they tend to offer to public prevention of private abuses. For example: if you don't like working a hundred hours a week for twenty-five cents a day, then find another employer! It is obvious to intelligent people, if not libertarians, that more generous employers will price themselves out of a market whose standards are set by the most rapacious.

-Michael Lind

Libertarians secretly worried that ultimately someone will figure out the whole of their political philosophy boils down to 'get off my property.' News flash: This is not really a big secret to the rest of us.

-John Scalzi

Libertarians sometimes prove that a foolish consistency is the hobgoblin of little minds, and that there is a difference between logic and wisdom.

-Molly Ivins

Liberty has never come from the government. Liberty has always come from the subjects of the government. The history of liberty is a history of resistance. The history of liberty is a history of the limitation of governmental power, not the increase of it.

-Woodrow Wilson

Liberty is not a means to a higher political end. It is itself the highest political end.

-John Dalberg-Acton

Life has many good things. The problem is that most of these good things can be gotten only by sacrificing other good things. We all recognize this in our daily lives. It is only in politics that this simple, common sense fact is routinely ignored.

-Thomas Sowell

Life is not fair, but government absolutely must be.
-*Ann Richards*

Like Lincoln, I would like to believe the ballot is stronger than the bullet. Then again, he said that before he got shot.
-*Sarah Vowell*

Like the effect of advertising upon the customer, the methods of political propaganda tend to increase the feeling of insignificance of the individual voter.
-*Erich Fromm*

Lobbyists are people who go to Washington to mix business with pressure.
-*Lane Olinghouse*

Lord, the money we do spend on Government and it's not one bit better than the government we got for one-third the money twenty years ago.
-*Will Rogers*

Love and business and family and religion and art and patriotism are nothing but shadows of words when a man's starving.
-*O. Henry*

Love your country, but never trust its government.
-*Robert A. Heinlein*

Loyalty in politics was simply devotion to the side which a man conceives to be his side, and which he cannot leave without danger to himself.
-*Anthony Trollope*

Magnanimity in politics is not seldom the truest wisdom; and a great empire and little minds go ill together.
-Edmund Burke

Major (political) parties have lived more for patronage than for principles; their goal has been to bind together a sufficiently large coalition of diverse interests to get into power; and once in power, to arrange sufficiently satisfactory compromises of interests to remain there.
-Richard Hofstadter

Majority rule only works if you're also considering individual rights. Because you can't have five wolves and one sheep voting on what to have for supper.
-Larry Flynt

Man is by nature a political animal.
-Aristotle

Man is the only animal that laughs and has a state legislature.
-Samuel Butler (Novelist, 1835-1902)

Man's capacity for justice makes democracy possible, but man's inclination to injustice makes democracy necessary.
-Reinhold Neibuhr

Management is the gate through which social and economic and political change, indeed change in every direction, is diffused through society.
-Robert McNamara

Mankind are governed more by their feelings than by reason.
-Samuel Adams

Many people consider the things government does for them to be social progress but they regard the things government does for others as socialism.
-*Earl Warren*

Many people find smoking objectionable. I myself find many- even more- things objectionable. I do not like aftershave lotion, adults who roller-skate, children who speak French, or anyone who is unduly tanned. I do not, however, go around enacting legislation and putting up signs.
-*Fran Lebowitz*

Many people, especially in government and business, assume the press is hostile, uninformed and likely to distort or sensationalize everything. Many reporters and editors, on the other hand, assume that everything secret is scandalous, and every claim of confidentiality is a cover-up.
-*Katharine Graham*

Many years ago, I concluded that a few hair shirts were part of the mental wardrobe of every man. The president differs from other men in that he has a more extensive wardrobe.
-*Herbert Hoover*

Mark my word, if and when these preachers get control of the (Republican) party, and they're sure trying to do so, it's going to be a terrible damn problem. Frankly, these people frighten me. Politics and governing demand compromise. But these Christians believe they are acting in the name of God, so they can't and won't compromise. I know, I've tried to deal with them.
-*Barry M. Goldwater*

Maybe a vague president and an incompetent and somewhat corrupt administration is what the nation needs.
-P.J. O'Rourke

Media people should have long noses like an elephant to smell out politicians, mayors, prime ministers and businessmen. We need to know the reality, the good and the bad, not just the appearance.
-Tenzin Gyatso (The 14th Dalai Lama)

Mediocrity triumphs because it presents itself as democratic and because it is dull, and so for many does not seem worth struggling against.
-Theodore Dalrymple

Men are conservatives when they are least vigorous, or when they are most luxurious. They are conservatives after dinner.
-Ralph Waldo Emerson

Men in authority will always think that criticism of their policies is dangerous. They will always equate their policies with patriotism, and find criticism subversive.
-Henry Steele Commager

Men make history, and not the other way around. In periods where there is no leadership, society stands still. Progress occurs when courageous, skillful leaders seize the opportunity to change things for the better.
-Harry S. Truman

Men may make laws to hinder and fetter the ballot, but men cannot make laws that will bind or retard the growth of manhood.
-Booker T. Washington

The Big Book of American Political Quotations

Men must turn square corners when they deal with the Government.
-*Oliver Wendell Holmes, Jr.*

Men well governed should seek after no other liberty, for there can be no greater liberty than a good government.
-*Sir Walter Raleigh*

Mere political reform will not cure the manifold evils which now afflict society. There requires a social reform, a domestic reform, an individual reform.
-*Samuel Smiles*

Minor (political) parties have been attached to some special idea or interest, and they have generally expressed their positions through firm and identifiable programs and principles. Their function has not been to win or govern, but to agitate, educate, generate new ideas, and supply the dynamic element in our political life. When a third party's demands become popular enough, they are appropriated by one or both of the major parties and the third party disappears. Third parties are like bees: once they have stung, they die.
-*Richard Hofstadter*

Misinformed is the new patriotic.
-*Chuck Lorre*

Moderate Republicans are reverse Houdinis. They tie themselves up in knots and then tell you they can't do anything because they're tied up in knots.
-*Barney Frank*

Modern Americans behave as if intelligence were some sort of hideous deformity.
-*Frank Zappa*

Modern politics is, at bottom, a struggle not of men but of forces.
-Henry Adams

Money alone determines your entire life, political as well as private.
-Germaine de Stael

Moral decay first hampers and then strangles honest government, regular commerce, and even the ability to take genuine pleasure in the goods of this world.
-Russell Kirk

Morality cannot be legislated, but behavior can be regulated. Judicial decrees may not change the heart, but they can restrain the heartless.
-Rev. Martin Luther King, Jr.

Morality has nothing in common with politics.
-Bob Dylan

More often than not Democratic Law works to the advantage of the few even though the many have voted; this, of course, is because the few have told them how to vote.
-Charles Bukowski

Most Americans aren't the sort of citizens the Founding Fathers expected; they are contented serfs. Far from being active critics of government, they assume that its might makes it right.
-Joseph Sobran

Most Americans hold a generous opinion of their own morals, even while they remain acutely aware of others' failings.
-David Whitman

Most Americans probably aren't aware that there was a time in this country when tanks and cavalry were massed on Pennsylvania Avenue to chase away the unemployed.
-*Andrew Grove*

Most libertarians are worried about government but not worried about business. I think we need to be worrying about business in exactly the same way we are worrying about government.
-*John Perry Barlow*

Most of all, I remember those children in the classrooms and those kids who grabbed me around the knees, and I think of the old people who really need a voice when they're trapped in wheelchairs in dirty nursing homes. The person in this office really must have a conscience to know that how they direct this government dramatically affects the lives of those people.
-*Ann Richards*

Most of the ladies and gentlemen who mourn the passing of the nation's leaders wouldn't know a leader if they saw one. If they had the bad luck to come across a leader, they would find out that he might demand something from them, and this impertinence would put an abrupt and indignant end to their wish for his return.
-*Lewis H. Lapham*

Most presidents are merely clerks of some real power which stands erect at their side and does its will by them.
-*Ralph Waldo Emerson*

Most social institutions seem to be designed to keep man in a state of intellectual and emotional mediocrity that makes him more fit to govern or be governed.
-*Nicolas Chamfort*

Mothers all want their sons to grow up to be President but they don't want them to become politicians in the process.
-*John F. Kennedy*

My ancestors were Puritans from England. They arrived here in 1648 in the hope of finding greater restrictions than were permissible under English law at that time.
-*Garrison Keillor*

My choice early in life was either to be a piano player in a whore-house or a politician. And to tell the truth, there's hardly any difference.
-*Harry S. Truman*

'My country, right or wrong' is a thing that no patriot would think of saying except in a desperate case. It is like saying 'My mother, drunk or sober.'
-*G.K. Chesterton*

My country, right or wrong. In one sense I say so too. My country; and my country is the great American Republic. My country, right or wrong; if right, to be kept right; and if wrong, to be set right.
-*Carl Schurz*

My faith in the people governing is, on the whole, infinitesimal; my faith in The People governed is, on the whole, illimitable.
-*Charles Dickens*

My father had a deep and lifelong contempt for politicians in general. 'They tell lies,' he used to say with wonder, 'even when they don't have to.'
-*Gore Vidal*

My father's view was that the public is the employer of these government employees and has the right to know what they're up to.
-Jack Anderson

My ideal citizen is the self-employed, homeschooling, IRA-owning guy with a concealed-carry permit. Because that person doesn't need the goddamn government for anything,
-Grover Norquist

My political ideal is democracy. Let every man be respected as an individual and no man idolized.
-Albert Einstein

My political life has been informed by the view that if there was any truth to religion there wouldn't really be any need for politics.
-Christopher Hitchens

National security includes schools for our children as well as silos for our missiles. It includes the health of our families as much as the size of our bombs, the safety of our streets, and the condition of our cities, and not just the engines of war. If we some day choke on the pollution of our own air, there will be little consolation in leaving behind a dying continent ringed with steel.
-George McGovern

National strength includes the credibility of our system in the eyes of our own people as well as the credibility of our deterrent in the eyes of others abroad.
-George McGovern

Nationalism of one kind or another was the cause of most of the genocide of the twentieth century. Flags are bits of colored cloth that governments use first to shrink-wrap people's brains and then as ceremonial shrouds to bury the dead.
-Arundhati Roy

Nations around the world look to us for leadership not merely by strength of arms, but by the strength of our convictions. We not only want, but we need, the free exercise of rights by every American. We need the strength and talent of ever American. We need, in short, to set an example of freedom for the world- and for ourselves.
-Robert F. Kennedy

Neither conservatives nor humorists believe man is good. But left-wingers do.
-P.J. O'Rourke

Never judge a country by its politicians.
-Alfred Hitchcock

Never pass up an opportunity to appear on C-Span. C-Span viewers vote.
-Lamar Alexander

Never vote for the best candidate. Vote for the one who will do the least harm.
-Frank Dane

Next time I tell you someone from Texas should not be president of the United States, please pay attention.
-Molly Ivins

Nil desperandum,- Never Despair. That is a motto for you and me. All are not dead; and where there is a spark of patriotic fire, we will rekindle it.
-*Samuel Adams*

Ninety percent of the politicians give the other ten percent a bad name.
-*Henry Kissinger*

Ninety-eight percent of the adults in this country are decent, hard working, honest Americans. It's the other lousy two percent that get all the publicity. But then, we elected them.
-*Lily Tomlin*

No amount of charters, direct primaries, or short ballots will make a democracy out of an illiterate people.
-*Walter Lippmann*

No class of Americans, so far as I know, has ever objected... to any amount of governmental meddling if it appeared to benefit that particular class.
-*Carl L. Becker*

No government can be long secure without formidable opposition.
-*Benjamin Disraeli*

No government could survive without champagne. Champagne in the throat of our diplomatic people is like oil in the wheels of an engine.
-*Joseph Dargent*

No government ought to be without censors: and where the press is free, no one ever will.
-*Thomas Jefferson*

No higher proof exists of the strength of popular government than, though the chosen of the people be struck down, his constitutional successor is peacefully installed without shock or strain.
-Chester A. Arthur

No man can be a patriot on an empty stomach.
-William Cowper Brann

No man is good enough to govern another man without that other's consent.
-Abraham Lincoln

No man is good enough to govern any woman without her consent.
-Susan B. Anthony

No man should advocate a course in private that he's ashamed to admit in public.
-George McGovern

No man who ever held the office of president would congratulate a friend on obtaining it. He will make one man ungrateful, and a hundred men his enemies, for every office he can bestow.
-John Adams

No man, however strong, can serve ten years as schoolmaster, priest, or Senator, and remain fit for anything else.
-Henry Adams

No matter how much the government controls the economic system, any problem will be blamed on whatever small zone of freedom that remains.
-Sheldon Richman

No one is innocent after the experience of governing. But not everyone is guilty.
-*Daniel Patrick Moynihan*

No party is as bad as its state and national leaders.
-*Will Rogers*

No politician is perfect. But in every election in your life, there will be one choice that is better than the others. Go out and vote for that one.
-*Bill Maher*

No protracted war can fail to endanger the freedom of a democratic country.
-*Alexis de Tocqueville*

No tyranny is so irksome as petty tyranny: the officious demands of policemen, government clerks, and electromechanical gadgets.
-*Edward Abbey*

No wonder scoundrels find refuge in patriotism; it offers them immunity from criticism.
-*Bill Moyers*

Nobody black or white who really believes in democracy can stand aside now; everybody's got to stand up and be counted.
-*Lena Horne*

Not long ago, if you wanted to seize political power in a country you had merely to control the army and the police. Today it is only in the most backward countries that fascist generals, in carrying out a coup d'état, still use tanks. If a country has reached a high degree of industrialization the whole scene changes. The day after the fall of Khrushchev, the editors of Pravda, Izvestiia, the heads of the radio and television were replaced; the army wasn't called out. Today a country belongs to the person who controls communications.
-*Umberto Eco*

Not only does democracy make every man forget his ancestors, but also clouds their view of their descendants and isolates them from their contemporaries. Each man is for ever thrown back on himself alone, and there is danger that he may be shut up in the solitude of his own heart.
-*Alexis de Tocqueville*

Not only does the action of Governments not deter men from crimes; on the contrary, it increases crime by always disturbing and lowering the moral standard of society.
-*Leo Tolstoy*

Nothing can astound an American. It has often been asserted that the word 'impossible' is not a French one. People have evidently been deceived by the dictionary. In America, all is easy, all is simple; and as for mechanical difficulties, they are overcome before they arise.
-*Jules Verne*

Nothing can so alienate a voter from the political system as backing a winning candidate.
-*Mark B. Cohen*

Nothing is irreparable in politics.
-*Jean Anouilh*

Nothing is more destructive of respect for the government and the law of the land than passing laws which cannot be enforced.
-*Albert Einstein*

Nothing is more surprising than the easiness with which the many are governed by the few.
-*David Hume*

Nothing is so admirable in politics as a short memory.
-*John Kenneth Galbraith*

Nothing is so permanent as a temporary government program.
-*Milton Friedman*

Nothing will upset a state economic condition like a legislature. It's better to have termites in your house than the legislature.
-*Will Rogers*

Now I know what a statesman is; he's a dead politician. We need more statesmen.
-*Bob Edwards*

Now and then an innocent man is sent to the legislature.
-*Frank McKinney (Kin) Hubbard*

Nowadays almost every business is like show business, including politics, which has become more like show business than show business is.
-*Russell Baker*

Numerous politicians have seized absolute power and muzzled the press. Never in history has the press seized absolute power and muzzled the politicians.
-*Otto von Bismarck*

Occasionally the vice president may make a difference, but rarely one that matters.
-*James Q. Wilson*

Of all sciences there is none where first appearances are more deceitful than in politics.
-*David Hume*

Of course politics is an interesting and engrossing thing. It offers no immutable laws, nearly always prevaricates, but as far as blather and sharpening the mind go, it provides inexhaustible material.
-*Anton Chekhov*

Of course the people don't want war. But after all, it's the leaders of the country who determine the policy, and it's always a simple matter to drag the people along whether it's a democracy, a fascist dictatorship, or a parliament, or a communist dictatorship. Voice or no voice, the people can always be brought to the bidding of the leaders. That is easy. All you have to do is tell them they are being attacked, and denounce the pacifists for lack of patriotism, and exposing the country to greater danger. (at the Nuremberg Trials)
-*Herman Goering*

Of course we're unilateral. If we Americans had wanted to be ordered around by English wig-tops, French functionaries, bossy Germans, disorganized Italians, tin-pot Latin American dictators, and Ice Age Siberian bureaucrats, we would have stayed where we were.
-*P.J. O'Rourke*

Of what does politics consist except the making of imperfect decisions, many of them unjust and quite a few of them deadly?
-*Lewis H. Lapham*

Oh, that lovely title, ex-President.
-*Dwight D. Eisenhower*

Old forms of government finally grow so oppressive, that they must be thrown off even at the risk of reigns of terror.
-*Herbert Spencer*

On *The Twilight Zone,* I knew that I could get away with Martians saying things that Republicans and Democrats couldn't.
-*Rod Serling*

On the one hand, the Republicans are telling industrial workers that the high cost of food in the cities is due to this government's farm policy. On the other hand, the Republicans are telling the farmers that the high cost of manufactured goods on the farm is due to this government's labor policy. That's plain hokum. It's an old political trick: 'If you can't convince 'em, confuse 'em.' But this time it won't work.
-*Harry S. Truman*

On the whole, I prefer not to be lectured on patriotism by those who keep offshore mail drops in order to avoid paying their taxes.
-*Molly Ivins*

Once a government is committed to the principle of silencing the voice of opposition, it has only one way to go, and that is down the path of increasingly repressive measures, until it becomes a source of terror to all its citizens and creates a country where everyone lives in fear.
-*Harry S. Truman*

Once there were two brothers: one ran away to sea, the other was elected Vice-President- and nothing was ever heard from either of them again.
-*Thomas Marshall*

Once wide coercive powers are given to governmental agencies for particular purposes, such powers cannot be effectively controlled by democratic assemblies.
-*Friedrich Hayek*

Once you begin to take yourself seriously as a leader or as a follower, as a modern or as a conservative, then you become a self-conscious, biting, and scratching little animal whose work is not of the slightest value or importance to anybody.
-*Virginia Woolf*

Once you put yourself in the hands of the government, you could end up in Utah.
-*Michael O'Donoghue*

One can be a great poet and be politically stupid.
-*Umberto Eco*

One can lead a nation only by helping it see a bright outlook. A leader is a dealer in hope.
-*Napoleon Bonaparte*

One cannot always be sure of the truth of what one hears if he happens to be President of the United States.
-*William Howard Taft*

One cannot legislate problems out of existence. It has been tried.
-*Norman Augustine*

One difference between a liberal and a pickpocket is that if you demand your money back from a pickpocket, he won't question your motives. (from the *National Review*)
-*Variously attributed*

One difference between democracy and tyranny is that tyranny when challenged does not suspend its principles.
-*Robert Brault*

One has the right to be wrong in a democracy.
-*Claude Pepper*

One man, one vote: A legal doctrine requiring that, from time to time, old gerrymanders be replaced with new ones. The object of this is the achievement of genuine democracy.
-*Poul Anderson*

One of the greatest attractions of patriotism- it fulfills our worst wishes. In the person of our nation we are able, vicariously, to bully and cheat. Bully and cheat, what's more, with a feeling that we are profoundly virtuous.
-*Aldous Huxley*

One of the greatest delusions in the world is the hope that the evils in this world are to be cured by legislation.
-*Thomas B. Reed*

One of the merits of democracy is quite obvious: it is perhaps the most charming form of government ever devised by man. The reason is not far to seek. It is based on propositions that are palpably not true- and what is not true, as everyone knows, is always immensely more fascinating and satisfying to the vast majority of men than what is true.
-*H.L. Mencken*

One of the necessary accompaniments of capitalism in a democracy is political corruption.
-Upton Sinclair

One of the penalties for refusing to participate in politics is that you end up being governed by your inferiors.
-Plato

One of these days the people of Louisiana are going to get good government- and they aren't going to like it.
-Huey P. Long

One person's act of political genius is another person's despicable betrayal of all that is dear.
-Sean Kelly

One thing you need never fear in a democracy is ignorance without representation.
-Robert Brault

One word sums up probably the responsibility of any vice president, and that one word is 'to be prepared.'
-Dan Quayle (vice president under George H.W. Bush)

One's right to life, liberty, and property, to free speech, a free press, freedom of worship and assembly, and other fundamental rights may not be submitted to vote; they depend on the outcome of no elections.
-Hugo Black

One, if one is sensible, blames government, not the servers of government, not those entangled in their governments.
-Taylor Caldwell

Only a government that is rich and safe can afford to be a democracy, for democracy is the most expensive and nefarious kind of government ever heard of on earth.
-*H.L. Mencken*

Only a knowledgeable, empowered and vocal citizenry can perform well in democracy.
-*David Brin*

Only in America can you be pro-death penalty, pro-war, pro-unmanned drone bombs, pro-nuclear weapons, pro-guns, pro-torture, pro-land mines, and still call yourself 'pro-life.'
-*John Fugelsang*

Only in America can you find so many angry people claiming to love their country, while hating almost anyone in it.
-*Don King*

Only in America would you have a war, get it over with and have all the heroes either be generals or politicians.
-*H. Ross Perot*

Only the Government, it seems, has a legal right to manipulate opinion with hot documents.
-*Russell Baker*

Only the emergency that makes it immediately dangerous to leave the correction of evil counsels to time warrants making any exception to the sweeping command, 'Congress shall make no law...abridging the freedom of speech.'
-*Oliver Wendell Holmes, Jr.*

Only the good die young, which explains the average age of Congressmen.
-Variously attributed

Organized greed always defeats disorganized democracy.
-Matt Taibbi

Other employees would do no better than Congressmen if the boss showed an interest in them only once in two years.
-Variously attributed

Our 'neoconservatives' are neither new nor conservative, but old as Babylon and evil as Hell.
-Edward Abbey

Our Constitution was not written in the sands to be washed away by each wave of new judges blown in by each successive political wind.
-Hugo Black

Our aims in political activism are not, and should not be, to create a perfect utopia. What we seek is more simply to improve the quality of human life while at the same time respecting the natural environment which sustains it: 'Not a heaven on earth but a better earth on earth.'
-Paul Wellstone

Our constitution protects aliens, drunks, and U.S. Senators. There ought to be one day (just one) when there is open season on senators.
-Will Rogers

Our country, of course, was born on the very simple idea that freedom is our only cause, and that freedom was not given to us by government.
-Barry M. Goldwater

Our definition of patriotism is often too narrow. Shall the lover of his country measure his loyalty only by his service as a soldier?
-*William Jennings Bryan*

Our elections are free, it's in the results where eventually we pay.
-*Bill Stern*

Our government has kept us in a perpetual state of fear- kept us in a continuous stampede of patriotic fervor- with the cry of grave national emergency. Always there has been some terrible evil at home or some monstrous foreign power that was going to gobble us up if we did not blindly rally behind it by furnishing the exorbitant funds demanded. Yet, in retrospect, these disasters seem never to have happened, seem never to have been quite real.
-*Douglas MacArthur*

Our government is the potent, the omnipresent teacher. For good or for ill, it teaches the whole people by its example.
-*Louis Brandeis*

Our government rests in public opinion. Whoever can change public opinion, can change the government, practically just so much.
-*Abraham Lincoln*

Our great democracies still tend to think that a stupid man is more likely to be honest than a clever man, and our politicians take advantage of this prejudice by pretending to be even more stupid than nature made them.
-*Bertrand Russell*

Our media and political system has turned into a mutual protection racket.
-*Bill Moyers*

Our most dangerous tendency is to expect too much of government, and at the same time do for it too little.
-*Warren G. Harding*

Our only hope is to control the vote.
-*Medgar Evers*

Our own free system to live and progress has to have intelligent citizens, citizens who cannot only think and speak and write to influence people, but citizens who are free to do that without fear of governmental censorship or reprisal.
-*Hugo Black*

Our political institutions work remarkably well. They are designed to clang against each other. The noise is democracy at work.
-*Michael Novak*

Our representative democracy is not working because the Congress that is supposed to represent the voters does not respond to their needs. I believe the chief reason for this is that it is ruled by a small group of old men.
-*Shirley Chisholm*

Our whole constitutional heritage rebels at the thought of giving government the power to control men's minds.
-*Thurgood Marshall*

Our whole way of life today is dedicated to the removal of risk. Cradle to grave we are supported, insulated, and isolated from the risks of life- and if we fail, our government stands ready with Bandaids of every size.
-*Shirley Temple*

The Big Book of American Political Quotations

Ours is a government of checks and balances. The Mafia and crooked businessmen make out checks, and the politicians and other compromised officials improve their bank balances.
-Steve Allen

Owning your own home is America's unique recipe for avoiding revolution and promoting pseudo-equality at the same time. To keep citizens puttering in their yards instead of sputtering on the barricades, the government has gladly deprived itself of billions in tax revenues by letting home 'owners' deduct mortgage interest payments.
-Florence King

Painful as it may be to hear it, there's nothing special about the people of this country that sets them apart from the other people of the world. It is the Bill of Rights, and only the Bill of Rights, that keeps us from becoming the world's biggest banana republic. The moment we forget that, the American Dream is over.
-Alexander Hope

Party leads to vicious, corrupt and unprofitable legislation, for the sole purpose of defeating party.
-James Fenimore Cooper

Party politics is the most narrow minded occupation in the world.
-Will Rogers

Patriotic duty and the disease of nationalism lure us to deny our common humanity.
-Chris Hedges

Patriotism ... is a superstition artificially created and maintained through a network of lies and falsehoods; a superstition that robs man of his self-respect and dignity, and increases his arrogance and conceit.
-*Emma Goldman*

Patriotism at the expense of another nation is as wicked as racism at the expense of another race. Let us resolve to be patriots always, nationalists never.
-*William Sloane Coffin, Jr.*

Patriotism calls for the faithful and conscientious performance of all of the duties of citizenship, in small matters as well as great, at home as well as upon the tented field.
-*William Jennings Bryan*

Patriotism is a kind of religion; it is the egg from which wars are hatched.
-*Guy de Maupassant*

Patriotism is a lively sense of collective responsibility. Nationalism is a silly cock crowing on its own dunghill.
-*Richard Aldington*

Patriotism is a pernicious, psychopathic form of idiocy.
-*George Bernard Shaw*

Patriotism is an ephemeral motive that scarcely ever outlasts the particular threat to society that aroused it.
-*Denis Diderot*

Patriotism is collective responsibility.
-*Arnold H. Glasow*

Patriotism is easy to understand in America. It means looking out for yourself by looking out for your country.
-*Calvin Coolidge*

Patriotism is largely pride, and very largely combativeness. Patriotism generally has a chip on its shoulder.
-*Charlotte Perkins Gilman*

Patriotism is not a short and frenzied outburst of emotion but the tranquil and steady dedication of a lifetime.
-*Adlai E. Stevenson II*

Patriotism is often an arbitrary veneration of real estate above principles.
-*George Jean Nathan*

Patriotism is only a virtue if the person who has it lives in your country.
-*Andy Rooney*

Patriotism is supporting your country all the time, and your government when it deserves it.
-*Mark Twain*

Patriotism is the last refuge of a scoundrel.
-*Samuel Johnson*

Patriotism is the religion of hell.
-*James Branch Cabell*

Patriotism is the virtue of the vicious.
-*Oscar Wilde*

Patriotism is the willingness to kill and be killed for trivial reasons.
-Bertrand Russell

Patriotism is usually stronger than class hatred, and always stronger than internationalism.
-George Orwell

Patriotism is when love of your own people comes first; nationalism, when hate for people other than your own comes first.
-Charles de Gaulle

Patriotism is your conviction that this country is superior to all others because you were born in it.
-George Bernard Shaw

Patriotism varies, from a noble devotion to a moral lunacy.
-William R. Inge

Patriotism, like religion, meets people's need for something greater to which their individual lives can be anchored... America's state religion, (is) patriotism, a phenomenon which has convinced many of the citizenry that 'treason' is morally worse than murder or rape.
-William Blum

Patriotism, red hot, is compatible with the existence of a neglect of national interests, a dishonesty, a cold indifference to the suffering of millions.
-Charlotte Perkins Gilman

Patriotism, when it wants to make itself felt in the domain of learning, is a dirty fellow who should be thrown out of doors.
-Arthur Schopenhauer

Patriotism. Combustible rubbish ready to the torch of any one ambitious to illuminate his name.
-Ambrose Bierce

Patriots always talk of dying for their country, and never of killing for their country.
-Bertrand Russell

Peace does not come rolling in on the wheels of inevitability. We can't just wish for peace. We have to will it, fight for it, suffer for it, demand it from our governments as if peace were God's most cherished hope for humanity, as indeed it is.
-William Sloane Coffin, Jr.

People expect Byzantine, Machiavellian logic from politicians. But the truth is simple. Trial lawyers learn a good rule: 'Don't decide what you don't have to decide.' That's not evasion, it's wisdom.
-Mario Cuomo

People never lie so much as after a hunt, during a war, or before an election.
-Otto von Bismarck

People use democracy as a free-floating abstraction disconnected from reality. Democracy in and of itself is not necessarily good. Gang rape, after all, is democracy in action.
-Terry Goodkind

People vote their resentment, not their appreciation. The average man does not vote for anything but against something.
-H.H. Munro Saki

People who are wise, good, smart, skillful, or hardworking don't need politics, they have jobs.
-*P.J. O'Rourke*

People who don't believe in government are likely to defile government.
-*Bill Moyers*

Peoples do never govern themselves. That lunacy was concocted by liberalism. Behind its 'people's sovereignty' the slyest cheaters are hiding, who don't want to be recognized.
-*Joseph Goebbels*

Permanent crisis justifies permanent control of everybody and everything by the agencies of central government.
-*Aldous Huxley*

Persuade your fellow citizens it's a good idea and pass a law. That's what democracy is all about. It's not about nine superannuated judges who have been there too. If you're going to be a good and faithful judge, you have to resign yourself to the fact that you're not always going to like the conclusions you reach. If you like.
-*Antonin Scalia*

Plato would have no actors in his republic, in case pretense devoured what was real. Plato's fears have proved well-grounded.
-*Brian Aldiss*

Plutocracy is abhorrent to a republic; it is more despotic than monarchy, more heartless than aristocracy, more selfish than bureaucracy. It preys upon the nation in time of peace and conspires against it in the hour of its calamity.
-*William Jennings Bryan*

Political abstractions can disguise or change the meaning of the most elementary realities.
-*Theodore Dalrymple*

Political campaigns are designedly made into emotional orgies which endeavor to distract attention from the real issues involved, and they actually paralyze what slight powers of cerebration man can normally muster.
-*James Harvey Robinson*

Political correctness is just tyranny with manners. I wish for you the courage to be unpopular. Popularity is history's pocket change. Courage is history's true currency.
-*Charlton Heston*

Political figures who talk a lot about liberty and freedom invariably turn out to mean the freedom to not pay taxes and discriminate based on race; freedom to hold different ideas and express them, not so much.
-*Paul Krugman*

Political language- and with variations this is true of all political parties, from Conservatives to Anarchists- is designed to make lies sound truthful and murder respectable, and to give an appearance of solidity to pure wind.
-*George Orwell*

Political organizations are formed to keep the powerful in power.
-*Shirley Chisholm*

Political questions are far too serious to be left to the politicians.
-*Hannah Arendt*

The Big Book of American Political Quotations

Political satire became obsolete when Henry Kissinger was awarded the Nobel Peace Prize.
-Tom Lehrer

Political success is the ability, when the inevitable occurs, to get credit for it.
-Laurence J. Peter

Politically popular speech has always been protected: even the Jews were free to say 'Heil Hitler.'
-Isaac Asimov

Politicians and diapers have one thing in common. They should both be changed regularly and for the same reason.
-Gerry Brooks

Politicians and journalists share the same fate in that they often understand tomorrow the things they talk about today.
-Helmut Schmidt

Politicians are actors, too, don't you think? Usually, if you like people and you're outgoing, not a shy little thing, you can do pretty well in politics.
-Shirley Temple

Politicians are always realistically maneuvering for the next election. They are obsolete as fundamental problem-solvers.
-Buckminster Fuller

Politicians are interested in people. Not that this is always a virtue. Fleas are interested in dogs.
-P.J. O'Rourke

The Big Book of American Political Quotations

Politicians are like bad horsemen who are so preoccupied with staying in the saddle that they can't bother about where they're going.
-Joseph A. Schumpeter

Politicians are like ships: noisiest when lost in a fog.
-Bennett Cerf

Politicians are people who, when they see light at the end of the tunnel, go out and buy some more tunnel.
-John Quinton

Politicians are swine. You cannot reason with swine. You must hit them on the nose with a stick.
-Bertolt Brecht

Politicians are the same the world over. They promise to build a bridge where there is no river.
-Nikita Kruschev

Politicians fascinate because they constitute such a paradox; they are an elite that accomplishes mediocrity for the public good.
-George F. Will

Politicians only get to the top because they have no qualifications to detain them at the bottom.
-Peter Ustinov

Politicians say they're beefing up our economy. Most don't know beef from pork.
-Harold Lowman

Politicians speak with great caution, since they must take care not to actually say anything.
-George Carlin

Politics and prostitution have to be the only jobs where inexperience is considered a virtue. In what other profession would you brag about not knowing stuff?
-Tina Fey

Politics and the shape of mankind are shaped by men without ideals and without greatness. Men who have greatness within them don't concern themselves with politics.
-Albert Camus

Politics are a lousy way for a free man to get things done. Politics are, like God's infinite mercy, a last resort.
-P.J. O'Rourke

Politics are almost as exciting as war, and quite as dangerous. In war, you can only be killed once, but in politics many times.
-Winston Churchill

Politics are not the task of a Christian.
-Dietrich Bonhoeffer

Politics are nothing but sand and gravel: it is art and life that feed us until we die. Everything else is ambition, hysteria or hatred.
-Louise Bogan

Politics are usually the executive expression of human immaturity.
-Vera Brittain

Politics cannot be a science, because in politics theory and practice cannot be separated, and the sciences depend upon their separation.
-W.H. Auden

Politics determines who has the power, not who has the truth.
-Paul Krugman

Politics has got so expensive that it takes lots of money to even get beat with.
-*Will Rogers*

Politics have no relation to morals.
-*Niccolò Machiavelli*

Politics in America is the binding secular religion.
-*Theodore H. White*

Politics in a democracy is, at the end, an educational process.
-*Arthur Schlesinger, Jr.*

Politics is a matter of choices, and a man doesn't set up the choices himself. And there is always a price to make a choice. You know that. You've made a choice, and you know how much it cost you. There is always a price.
-*Robert Penn Warren*

Politics is a pendulum whose swings between anarchy and tyranny are fueled by perpetually rejuvenated illusions.
-*Albert Einstein*

Politics is a process which should slowly bring to public all the private worries and hopes of the individual.
-*Theodore H. White*

Politics is a science. You can demonstrate that you are right and that others are wrong.
-*Jean-Paul Sartre*

Politics is a strong and slow boring of hard boards.
-*Max Weber*

The Big Book of American Political Quotations

Politics is about compromises... really stupid compromises.
-Bill Maher

Politics is about who wins and loses. The rest is of marginal interest.
-Sean Wilentz

Politics is an act of faith; you have to show some kind of confidence in the intellectual and moral capacity of the public.
-George McGovern

Politics is applied biology.
-Ernst Haeckel

Politics is developing more comedians than radio ever did.
-Jimmy Durante

Politics is downstream from culture.
-Andrew Breitbart

Politics is how you live your life, not whom you vote for.
-Jerry Rubin

Politics is just like show business, you have a hell of an opening, coast for a while and then have a hell of a close.
-Ronald Reagan

Politics is knowing when to pull the trigger.
-Variously attributed

Politics is like a race horse. A good jockey must know how to fall with the least possible damage.
-Edouard Herriot

Politics is like navigation in a sea without charts, and wise men live the lives of pilgrims.
-*Joyce Carey*

Politics is like the bumper cars at the amusement park. It's a delusion to think that by refusing to move, you can protect yourself from being hit.
-*from The Weekly Standard.*

Politics is like the stock market: it's a bad business for people who can't afford to lose.
-*Richard M. Nixon*

Politics is made up largely of irrelevancies.
-*Dalton Camp*

Politics is not a bad profession. If you succeed there are many rewards, if you disgrace yourself you can always write a book.
-*Ronald Reagan*

Politics is not about winning for the sake of winning.
-*Paul Wellstone*

Politics is not an exact science.
-*Otto von Bismarck*

Politics is not just about power and money games, politics can be about the improvement of people's lives, about lessening human suffering in our world and bringing about more peace and more justice.
-*Paul Wellstone*

Politics is not predictions and politics is not observations. Politics is what we do. Politics is what we do, politics is what we create, by what we work for, by what we hope for and what we dare to imagine.
-*Paul Wellstone*

Politics is not the art of the possible. It consists in choosing between the disastrous and the unpalatable.
-*John Kenneth Galbraith*

Politics is organized hatred, that is unity.
-*John Jay Chapman*

Politics is perhaps the only profession for which no preparation is thought necessary.
-*Robert Louis Stevenson*

Politics is show business for ugly people.
-*Sonny Bono*

Politics is supposed to be the second oldest profession. I have come to realize that it bears a very close resemblance to the first.
-*Ronald Reagan*

Politics is the art of controlling your environment.
-*Hunter S. Thompson*

Politics is the art of looking for trouble, finding it whether it exists or not, diagnosing it incorrectly, and applying the wrong remedy.
-*Ernest Benn*

Politics is the art of postponing decisions until they are no longer relevant.
-*Henri Queuille*

The Big Book of American Political Quotations

Politics is the art of preventing people from taking part in affairs which properly concern them.
-Paul Valery

Politics is the art of the possible.
-Otto von Bismarck

Politics is the business of getting power and privilege without possessing merit.
-P.J. O'Rourke

Politics is the conduct of public affairs for private advantage.
-Ambrose Bierce

Politics is the gentle art of getting votes from the poor and campaign funds from the rich by promising to protect each from the other.
-Oscar Ameringer

Politics is the only field of human endeavor where the more experience you have, the worse you get.
-Kinky Friedman

Politics is the pursuit of trivial men who, when they succeed at it, become important in the eyes of more trivial men.
-George Jean Nathan

Politics is the science of urgencies.
-Theodore Parker

Politics is the science of who gets what, when, and why.
-Sidney Hillman

The Big Book of American Political Quotations

Politics is the skilled use of blunt objects.
-*Lester B. Pearson*

Politics is too partisan, and sometimes patriotism is cast aside. Patriotism is honor and love of your country and your brothers and sisters. With politics I get the impression that it's all about what's good for the party and not necessarily what's good for the country.
-*Ricardo Montalbán*

Politics is very much like taxes- everybody is against them, or everybody is for them as long as they don't apply to him.
-*Fiorello LaGuardia*

Politics is war without bloodshed, while war is politics with bloodshed.
-*Mao Tse-tung*

Politics isn't about left versus right; it's about top versus bottom.
-*Jim Hightower*

Politics makes estranged bedfellows.
-*Goodman Ace*

Politics makes me uptight; I have so little control over it. It's like forever being in high school with rah-rah idiots in charge.
-*Rudy Rucker*

Politics means striving to share power or striving to influence the distribution of power, either among states or among groups within a state.
-*Max Weber*

Politics ruins the character.
-*Otto von Bismarck*

Politics should be limited in scope to war, protection of property, and the occasional precautionary beheading of a member of the ruling class.
-P.J. O'Rourke

Politics should share one purpose with religion: the steady emancipation of the individual through the education of his passions.
-George F. Will

Politics, as a practice, whatever its professions, has always been the systematic organization of hatreds.
-Henry Adams

Politics, it seems to me, for years, or all too long, has been concerned with right or left instead of right or wrong.
-Richard Armour

Politics, n. Strife of interests masquerading as a contest of principles.
-Ambrose Bierce

Politics: a Trojan horse race.
-Stanislaw J. Lec

Politics: the art of keeping as many balls as possible up in the air at one time- while protecting your own.
-Sam Attlesey

Politics: where fat, bald, disagreeable men, unable to be candidates themselves, teach a president how to act on a public stage.
-Jimmy Breslin

Polling is merely an instrument for gauging public opinion. When a president or any other leader pays attention to poll results, he is, in effect, paying attention to the views of the people. Any other interpretation is nonsense.
-George Gallup

Populism is always pandering, and pandering is always the reverse of leadership.
-George F. Will

Power is so pleasant that men quickly learn to be greedy in the enjoyment of it, and to flatter themselves that patriotism requires them to be imperious.
-Anthony Trollope

Practical politics consists of ignoring facts.
-Henry Adams

President Bush has said that he does not need approval from the UN to wage war, and I'm thinking, well, hell, he didn't need the approval of the American voters to become president, either.
-David Letterman

Presidential candidates don't chew gum.
-Theodore (Ted) Sorensen

Presidents come and go, but the Supreme Court goes on forever.
-William Howard Taft

Problem-solving leaders have one thing in common: a faith that there's always a better way.
-Gerald Weinberg

Professionals in a campaign are servants; they can tell him only how to do something once he tells them what it is he wants to do.
-*Theodore H. White*

Prosperity destroys fools and endangers the wise.
-*George Washington*

Protection and patriotism are reciprocal.
-*John C. Calhoun*

Protocol is etiquette with a government expense account.
-*Judith Martin*

Public confidence in the integrity of the Government is indispensable to faith in democracy; and when we lose faith in the system, we have lost faith in everything we fight and spend for.
-*Adlai E. Stevenson II*

Public education is a great instrument of social change. Through it, if we so desire, we can make our country more nearly a democracy without classes.
-*James Bryant Conant*

Punishment is now unfashionable... because it creates moral distinctions among men, which, to the democratic mind, are odious. We prefer a meaningless collective guilt to a meaningful individual responsibility.
-*Thomas Szasz*

Punishment is the last and least effective instrument in the hands of the legislator for the prevention of crime.
-*John Ruskin*

Reader, suppose you were an idiot. And suppose you were a member of Congress. But I repeat myself.
-*Mark Twain*

Real leaders must be ready to sacrifice all for the freedom of their people.
-*Nelson Mandela*

Real liberty is neither found in despotism or the extremes of democracy, but in moderate governments.
-*Alexander Hamilton*

Real politics are the possession and distribution of power.
-*Benjamin Disraeli*

Reality has a well-known liberal bias.
-*Stephen Colbert*

Reality is always more conservative than ideology.
-*Raymond Aron*

Regardless of how much blather you hear about the two parties bickering in Washington, the Beltway is really a monoculture that accommodates the two poles of a debate but very little in between.
-*David Carr*

Rehab is a failure if you come out of it and you're still a politician.
-*Andy Borowitz*

Relax, enjoy yourself. Have another drink. It's patriotic to overconsume.
-*Brian Aldiss*

Religion and government will both exist in greater purity, the less they are mixed together.
-*James Madison*

Religion is organized to satisfy and guide the soul- politics does the same thing for the body.
-*Joyce Carey*

Religion is so frequently a source of confusion in political life, and so frequently dangerous to democracy, precisely because it introduces absolutes into the realm of relative values.
-*Reinhold Neibuhr*

Religions are manipulated in order to serve those who govern society and not the other way around.
-*Gore Vidal*

Relying on the government to protect your privacy is like asking a peeping tom to install your window blinds.
-*John Perry Barlow*

Remember one thing about democracy. We can have anything we want and at the same time, we always end up with exactly what we deserve.
-*Edward Albee*

Remember, democracy never lasts long. It soon wastes, exhausts, and murders itself. There never was a democracy yet that did not commit suicide.
-*John Adams*

Remember, write to your Congressman. Even if he can't read, write to him.
-*Will Rogers*

Reporters are not there to curry presidential favor, nor can we respond to efforts at presidential intimidation. Our priority is the peoples' right to know- without fear or favor. We are the peoples' servants.
-Helen Thomas

Republicans are afraid someone, somewhere, might be having fun. Democrats are afraid someone, somewhere, might be making money.
-Variously attributed

Republicans are against abortion until their daughters need one, Democrats are for abortion until their daughter wants one.
-Grace McGarvie

Republicans are sore losers even when they win.
-Kevin G. Barkes

Republicans find libertarians convenient whenever they want to score some coke.
-Mark Russell

Republicans might be heathens and out to destroy all that we hold dear, but that doesn't mean we need to take them seriously. Or be bitter or vituperative just because they are swine. I think one can still have friends who are Republicans.
-Garrison Keillor

Republicans say that Democrats want a huge, monolithic federal institution that will compromise personal liberty and freedom by controlling individuals' lives with intrusive policies and a dictatorial agenda. Republicans, of course, believe that is the job of organized religion.
-Dennis Miller

Republicans want smaller government for the same reason crooks want fewer cops: it's easier to get away with murder.
-James Carville

Republics end through luxury, monarchies through poverty.
-Charles Louis de Montesquieu

Rich people march on Washington every day.
-I.F. Stone

Right now, there is a whole, an entire generation that never knew anything that didn't come out of this tube! This tube is the gospel, the ultimate revelation; this tube can make or break presidents, popes, prime ministers; this tube is the most awesome goddamn propaganda force in the whole godless world, and woe is us if it ever falls into the hands of the wrong people. (spoken by Peter Finch as Howard Beale in *Network*)
-Paddy Chayefsky

Ronald Reagan has held the two most demeaning jobs in the country-President of the United States and radio broadcaster for the Chicago Cubs.
-George F. Will

Rooting in work is crucial to any accomplishment. Rooting in mere enthusiasm will in the long run force illusory measures to keep the fires of empty enthusiasm going. And this makes politics and politicians.
-Wilhelm Reich

Rulers who wished to subvert the public liberty, may have found an established Clergy convenient auxiliaries. A just Government instituted to secure and perpetuate it needs them not.
-James Madison

The Big Book of American Political Quotations

Saying you have a political solution is like saying you can write a pop song that's going to stay at the top of the list forever.
-*Bruce Sterling*

Scarcely any political question arises in the United States that is not resolved, sooner or later, into a judicial question.
-*Alexis de Tocqueville*

Schools should be incredibly expensive for government and absolutely free of charge for its citizens, just like national defense. (Dialogue from *The West Wing*)
-*Aaron Sorkin*

Secrecy is an instrument of conspiracy; it ought not, therefore, to be the system of a regular government.
-*Jeremy Bentham*

See yourself as you really are. Listen to what none of your leaders and representatives dares tell you: You are a 'little, common man.' Understand the double meaning of these words: 'little' and 'common.'
-*Wilhelm Reich*

Self-esteem is the basis of any democracy.
-*Gloria Steinem*

Senators are a prolific source of advice, most of it bad.
-*Dean Acheson*

Separate is not equal. Duh.
-*Rachel Maddow*

Serial seduction, that's what politics is.
-*Richard Reeves*

Sex and politics are a lot alike. You don't have to be good at them to enjoy them.
-Barry M. Goldwater

Should any political party attempt to abolish social security, unemployment insurance, and eliminate labor laws and farm programs, you would not hear of that party again in our political history. There is a tiny splinter group, of course, that believes you can do these things... a few other Texas oil millionaires, and an occasional politician or business man from other areas. Their number is negligible and they are stupid.
-Dwight D. Eisenhower

Since a politician never believes what he says, he is always astonished when others do.
-Charles de Gaulle

Since governments take the right of death over their people, it is not astonishing if the people should sometimes take the right of death over governments.
-Guy de Maupassant

Sir, I wish to understand the true principles of the Government. I wish them carried out. I ask nothing more.
-William Henry Harrison

Sloths move at the speed of congressional debate but with greater deliberation and less noise.
-P.J. O'Rourke

So let us stand for justice and jobs and against special privilege.
-George McGovern

So long as all is ordered for attack, and that alone, leaders will instinctively increase the number of enemies that they may give their followers something to do.
-William Butler Yeats

So long as governments set the example of killing their enemies, private citizens will occasionally kill theirs.
-Elbert Hubbard

So long as we have enough people in this country willing to fight for their rights, we'll be called a democracy.
-Roger Nash Baldwin

So much money is being spent on the campaigns that I doubt if either man, as good as they are, are worth what it will cost to elect them.
-Will Rogers

So now is the time, more than ever, for those who truly value all the principles of democracy, especially including dissent, to be the most forceful in speaking up, standing up and speaking out.
-Jim Hightower

So who's perfect? Washington had false teeth. Franklin was near-sighted. Mussolini had syphilis. Unpleasant things have been said about Walt Whitman and Oscar Wilde. Tchaikovsky had his problems, too. And Lincoln was constipated.
-John O'Hara

Social conservatism and neoconservatism have revived authoritarian conservatism, and not for the better of conservatism or American democracy. True conservatism is cautious and prudent. Authoritarianism is rash and radical. American democracy has benefited from true conservatism, but authoritarianism offers potentially serious trouble for any democracy.
-*John Dean*

Social justice is a semantic fraud from the same stable as 'People's Democracy.'
-*Charles Curran*

Society in every state is a blessing, but government, even in its best state, is but a necessary evil; in its worst state an intolerable one.
-*Thomas Paine*

Soldiers are required to do their jobs when politicians fail to do theirs.
-*Peter P. Mahoney*

Some bastards have been great presidents.
-*Gore Vidal*

Some fellows get credit for being conservative when they are only stupid.
-*Frank McKinney (Kin) Hubbard*

Some guy tells you something. He says that's a national security matter. Well, you're supposed to tremble and get scared and it never, almost never means the security of the national government. More likely to mean the security or the personal happiness of the guy who is telling you something.
-*Ben Bradlee*

The Big Book of American Political Quotations

Some members of Congress are among the best actors in the world.
-Shirley Chisholm

Some people like to eat octopus. Liberals, mostly.
-Russell Baker

Some politician some years ago said that bad officials are elected by good voters who do not vote.
-Dwight D. Eisenhower

Some things I think are very conservative, or very liberal. I think when someone falls into one category for everything, I'm very suspicious. It doesn't make sense to me that you'd have the same solution to every issue.
-Louis C.K.

Somehow liberals have been unable to acquire from life what conservatives seem to be endowed with at birth: namely, a healthy skepticism of the powers of government agencies to do good.
-Daniel Patrick Moynihan

Sometimes I wonder if I'm patriotic enough. Yes, I want to kill people, but on both sides.
-Jack Handey

Sometimes I wonder if we shall ever grow up in our politics and say definite things which mean something, or whether we shall always go on using generalities to which everyone can subscribe, and which mean very little.
-Eleanor Roosevelt

Sometimes the news from Washington forces me to the conclusion that your mother and your brother Ed are in charge.
-James Thurber (cartoon caption)

The Big Book of American Political Quotations

Somewhere in Australia, a bunch of kangaroos are bitching about the bad reputation the Republicans are giving their court system.
-Paul Begala

Son, if you can't take their money, drink their whiskey, screw their women, and then vote against 'em, you don't deserve to be here.
-Sam Rayburn

Son, in politics you've got to learn that overnight chicken shit can turn to chicken salad.
-Lyndon B. Johnson

Standing armies are the oppressive instruments for governing the people, in the hands of hereditary and arbitrary monarchs.
-Daniel Webster

Standing up to your government can mean standing up for your country.
-Bill Moyers

Statesmanship is harder than politics. Politics is the art of getting along with people, whereas statesmanship is the art of getting along with politicians.
-Fletcher Knebel

Statesmen stand out because politicians are as alike as peas.
-Arnold H. Glasow

Stop tolerating in your leaders what you would not tolerate in your friends.
-Michael Ventura

Strongly guarded as is the separation between religion and government in the Constitution of the United States the danger of encroachment by Ecclesiastical Bodies, may be illustrated by precedents already furnished in their short history.
-*James Madison*

Stupidity cannot be cured with money, or through education, or by legislation.
-*Robert A. Heinlein*

Success in almost any field depends more on energy and drive than it does on intelligence. This explains why we have so many stupid leaders.
-*Sloan Wilson*

Success makes men rigid and they tend to exalt stability over all the other virtues; tired of the effort of willing they become fanatics about conservatism.
-*Walter Lippmann*

Surely human affairs would be far happier if the power in men to be silent were the same as that to speak. But experience more than sufficiently teaches that men govern nothing with more difficulty than their tongues.
-*Baruch Spinoza*

TV in America created the most coherent reality distortion field that I've ever seen. Therein is the problem: People who vote watch TV, and they are hallucinating like a sonofabitch. Basically, what we have in this country is government by hallucinating mob.
-*John Perry Barlow*

The Big Book of American Political Quotations

Take away the right to say 'fuck' and you take away the right to say 'fuck the government.'
-Lenny Bruce

Talk is cheap, except when Congress does it.
-Cullen Hightower

Television has made dictatorship impossible, but democracy unbearable.
-Shimon Peres

Television is democracy at its ugliest.
-Paddy Chayefsky

Television is the first truly democratic culture- the first culture available to everybody and entirely governed by what the people want. The most terrifying thing is what the people do want.
-Clive Barnes

Television is the most perfect democracy. You sit there with your remote control and vote.
-Aaron Brown

Terms like 'liberty' and 'individual freedom' invoked by generations of Americans who battled to widen the 1787 promise to 'promote the general welfare' have been perverted to create a government primarily dedicated to the state and the political class that runs it.
-Bill Moyers

Thanks to TV and for the convenience of TV, you can only be one of two kinds of human beings, either a liberal or a conservative.
-Kurt Vonnegut, Jr.

That government is best which governs the least, because its people discipline themselves.
-Thomas Jefferson

That's libertarians for you- anarchists who want police protection from their slaves.
-Kim Stanley Robinson

That's one of the major lessons: no president should ever take this nation to war without full public debate in the Congress and/or in the public.
-Robert McNamara

That's one thing about Republican Presidents. They never went in much for plans. They only had one plan. It says 'Boys, my head is turned. Just get it while you can.'
-Will Rogers

The American Constitution is the greatest governing document, and at some 7,000 words, just about the shortest.
-Stephen Ambrose

The American Republic will endure until the day Congress discovers that it can bribe the public with the public's money.
-Alexis de Tocqueville

The American government is premised on the theory that if the mind of man is to be free, his ideas, his beliefs, his ideology, his philosophy, must be placed beyond the reach of government.
-William O. Douglas

The American people are sick and tired of this 'lesser evil' garbage they get fed every election year. Both the Democrats and the Republicans do the same evils once they're in office.
-Roseanne Barr

The American people need no course in philosophy or political science or church history to know that God should not be made into a celestial party chairman.
-Mario Cuomo

The American people want to know that when they borrow a book from the library or buy a book, the government won't be looking over their shoulder. Everybody wants to fight terrorism, but we have to do it in a way that protects American freedom.
-Bernie Sanders

The American polity is infected with a serious imbalance of power between elites and masses, a power which is the principal threat to our democracy.
-Paul Wellstone

The American, if he has a spark of national feeling, will be humiliated by the very prospect of a foreigner's visit to Congress- these, for the most part, illiterate hacks whose fancy vests are spotted with gravy, and whose speeches, hypocritical, unctuous and slovenly, are spotted also with the gravy of political patronage, these persons are a reflection on the democratic process rather than of it; they expose it in its underwear.
-Mary McCarthy

The Big Book of American Political Quotations

The Bill of Rights does not come from the people and is not subject to change by majorities. It comes from the nature of things. It declares the inalienable rights of man not only against all government but also against the people collectively.
-*Walter Lippmann*

The Bill of Rights was not written to protect governments from trouble. It was written precisely to give the people the constitutional means to cause trouble for governments they no longer trusted.
-*Henry Steele Commager*

The climate is just like it always was. Hot in the summer, cold in the winter and brainless in Washington.
-*Steve Goddard*

The common and continual mischiefs of the spirit of party are sufficient to make it the interest and duty of a wise people to discourage and restrain it.
-*George Washington*

The Constitution is not neutral. It was designed to take the government off the backs of people.
-*William O. Douglas*

The Constitution was framed fundamentally as a bulwark against governmental power, and preventing the arbitrary administration of punishment is a basic ideal of any society that purports to be governed by the rule of law.
-*William J. Brennan, Jr.*

The Democrats and Republicans are the same guy admiring himself in the mirror.
-*Kinky Friedman*

The Democrats don't want anyone to be born, but if you are, they will take care of you from the cradle to the grave. The Republicans don't mind if you are born, if you assure them that you don't plan to live long enough to collect your Social Security.
-Mort Sahl

The Egyptians of the First Dynasty were already civilized in most respects. They had hieroglyphics, metal weapons for killing foreigners, numerous government officials, death, and taxes.
-Will Cuppy

The First Amendment is often inconvenient. But that is besides the point. Inconvenience does not absolve the government of its obligation to tolerate speech.
-Anthony Kennedy

The First Amendment is truly the heart of the Bill of Rights. The Framers balanced its freedoms of religion, speech, press, assembly and petition against the needs of a powerful central government, and decided that in those freedoms lies this nation's only true security. They were not afraid for men to be free. We should not be.
-Hugo Black

The Framers of the Bill of Rights did not purport to create rights. Rather, they designed the Bill of Rights to prohibit our Government from infringing rights and liberties presumed to be preexisting.
-William J. Brennan, Jr.

The Government cannot afford to have a country made up entirely of rich people, because rich people pay so little tax that the Government would quickly go bankrupt. This is why Government men always tell us that labor is man's noblest calling. Government needs labor to pay its upkeep.
-Russell Baker

The Big Book of American Political Quotations

The Government of the absolute majority instead of the Government of the people is but the Government of the strongest interests; and when not efficiently checked, it is the most tyrannical and oppressive that can be devised.
-John C. Calhoun

The IRS sent back my tax return saying I owed $800. I said, 'If you'll remember, I fastened my return with a paper clip... which, according to your own very latest government Pentagon spending figures, will more than make up the difference.'
-Emo Philips

The Internet is democracy's revenge on democracy.
-Molly Haskell

The moral arc of a Washington career could be divided into four parts: idealism, pragmatism, ambition and corruption.
-Michael Kinsley

The National Government will regard it as its first and foremost duty to revive in the nation the spirit of unity and cooperation. It will preserve and defend those basic principles on which our nation has been built. It regards Christianity as the foundation of our national morality, and the family as the basis of national life...
-Adolf Hitler

The President has kept all of the promises he intended to keep. (as Bill Clinton's press secretary)
-George Stephanopoulos

The President has only 190 million bosses. The Vice President has 190 million and one.
-Hubert H. Humphrey

The President is always abused. If he isn't, he's doing nothing, and is of no value as the Chief Executive.
-*Harry S. Truman*

The President is merely the most important among a large number of public servants. He should be supported or opposed exactly to the degree which is warranted by his good conduct or bad conduct, his efficiency or inefficiency in rendering loyal, able, and disinterested service to the Nation as a whole. Therefore it is absolutely necessary that there should be full liberty to tell the truth about his acts, and this means that it is exactly necessary to blame him when he does wrong as to praise him when he does right. Any other attitude in an American citizen is both base and servile. To announce that there must be no criticism of the President, or that we are to stand by the President, right or wrong, is not only unpatriotic and servile, but is morally treasonable to the American public. Nothing but the truth should be spoken about him or any one else. But it is even more important to tell the truth, pleasant or unpleasant, about him than about any one else.
-*Theodore Roosevelt*

The President is the last person in the world to know what the people really want and think.
-*James A. Garfield*

The President is the people's lobbyist.
-*Hubert H. Humphrey*

The President must be greater than anyone else, but not better than anyone else. We subject him and his family to close and constant scrutiny and denounce them for things that we ourselves do every day. A Presidential slip of the tongue, a slight error in judgment- social, political, or ethical- can raise a storm of protest. We give the President more work than a man can do, more responsibility than a man should take, more pressure than a man can bear. We abuse him often and rarely praise him. We wear him out, use him up, eat him up. And with all this, Americans have a love for the President that goes beyond loyalty or party nationality; he is ours, and we exercise the right to destroy him.
-John Steinbeck

The Republican and Democratic parties, or, to be more exact, the Republican-Democratic party, represent the capitalist class in the class struggle. They are the political wings of the capitalist system and such differences as arise between them relate to spoils and not to principles.
-Eugene V. Debs

The Republican form of government is the highest form of government; but because of this it requires the highest type of human nature- a type nowhere at present existing.
-Herbert Spencer

The Republicans are against every piece of legislation that would benefit working Americans. Why do they oppose raising the minimum wage, pay equity for women, ending our disastrous unfettered free trade policies and expanding Social Security? Government is supposed to represent all Americans, not just the billionaire class.
-Bernie Sanders

The Republicans are coming- make nice.
-Ed Koch

The Republicans are the party that says government doesn't work; then they get elected and prove it.
-*P.J. O'Rourke*

The Republicans believe the wagon train will not make it to the frontier unless some of our old, some of our young, and some of our weak are left behind by the side of the trail. We Democrats believe that we can make it all the way with the whole family intact.
-*Mario Cuomo*

The Republicans favor a minimum wage- the smaller the minimum the better.
-*Harry S. Truman*

The Republicans in Congress lost their way. They swapped principle for power. They ended up with neither. They deserved to lose.
-*Alan Greenspan*

The Republicans' idea of 'right to life' begins at conception and ends at birth.
-*Barney Frank*

The Republicans, with their crazed Reagan fixation, are a last-gasp party, living posthumously, fighting battles on sex, race, immigration and public education long ago won by the other side. They're trying to roll back the clock, but time is passing them by.
-*Maureen Dowd*

The Republicans... are having a hard time getting their members to act as a unit instead of like a bunch of six-year-olds playing anarchist soccer; three teams, two goals, you decide.
-*Rachel Maddow*

The Senate being tied is a start. Now if only it could be gagged.
-*Bob Thaves*

The Senate is a place filled with goodwill and good intentions, and if the road to hell is paved with them, then it's a pretty good detour.
-*Hubert H. Humphrey*

The Senate is just what the mode of its election and the conditions of public life in this country make it.
-*Woodrow Wilson*

The Senate is the last primitive society in the world. We still worship the elders of the tribe and honor the territorial imperative.
-*Eugene McCarthy*

The Senate seems like the place where smart people go to die.
-*Jon Stewart*

The Supreme Court has ruled that they cannot have a nativity scene in Washington, DC. This wasn't for any religious reasons. They couldn't find three wise men and a virgin.
-*Jay Leno*

The Tea Party movement proves that all politics is yokel.
-*Christopher Hitchens*

The US, for historical reasons, mistrusts the concept of a welfare state, and this mistrust shows itself nakedly under present US government, which commits uncounted billions of the national wealth to what it calls defense, and is close-fisted in giving money to plans which would ameliorate the grinding poverty of a great part of its people. Quite simply, in Canada you could not get away with that.
-*Robertson Davies*

The United States Congress, like a lot of rich people, lives in two houses.
-John Green

The United States is only one superpower. Today they lead the world. Nobody has doubts about it. Militarily. They also lead economically but they're getting weak. But they don't lead morally and politically anymore. The world has no leadership. The United States was always the last resort and hope for all other nations. There was the hope, whenever something was going wrong, one could count on the United States. Today, we lost that hope.
-Lech Walesa

The White House has always attracted the mentally ill.
-(unidentified Secret Service agent)

The White House is the finest jail in the world.
-Harry S. Truman

The White House used to belong to the American people. At least that's what I learned from history books and from covering every president starting with John F. Kennedy. But now the 201-year-old Executive Mansion belongs only to a select, elitist group of people, including top government officials, members of Congress and the press corps. They and some others, all of whom are screened in advance, are welcome. But most people are not- not anymore.
-Helen Thomas

The accumulation of all powers, Legislative, Executive, and Judiciary, in the same hands, whether of one, a few, or many, and whether hereditary, self-appointed, or elective, may justly be pronounced the very definition of tyranny.
-James Madison

The Big Book of American Political Quotations

The aim of any good constitution is to achieve in a society a high degree of political harmony, so that order and justice and freedom may be maintained.
-Russell Kirk

The aim of constitutional government is to preserve the Republic; that of revolutionary government is to lay its foundation.
-Maximilien Robespierre

The argument for world government as the indispensable condition of world peace can be boiled down to a single proposition: if local civil government is necessary for local civil peace, then world civil government is necessary for world peace.
-Mortimer J. Adler

The art of governing consists simply of being honest, exercising common sense, following principle, and doing what is right and just.
-Thomas Jefferson

The art of politics consists in knowing precisely when it is necessary to hit an opponent slightly below the belt.
-Konrad Adenauer

The art of politics is ostentatious giving and surreptitious taking.
-Robert J. Vaughn

The awareness that we are all human beings together has become lost in war and through politics.
-Albert Schweitzer

The ballot is stronger than bullets.
-Joseph A. Schumpeter

The basic human rights documents- the American Declaration of Independence and the French Declaration of the Rights of Man- were written by political, not by religious, leaders.
-Arthur Schlesinger, Jr.

The basic political division in this country is not between liberals and conservatives but between those who believe that they should have a say in the love lives of strangers and those who do not.
-Judith Martin

The basis of effective government is public confidence and that confidence is endangered when ethical standards falter, or appear to falter.
-John F. Kennedy

The basis of our political systems is the right of the people to make and to alter their Constitutions of Government. But the Constitution which at any time exists, till changed by an explicit and authentic act of the whole people, is sacredly obligatory upon all.
-George Washington

The bed is now as public as the dinner table and governed by the same rules of formal confrontation.
-Angela Carter

The best argument against democracy is a five-minute conversation with the average voter.
-Variously attributed

The best conservatives can often give lessons to the liberals in true liberality of spirit, but the Fundamentalist program is essentially illiberal and intolerant.
-Harry Emerson Fosdick

The Big Book of American Political Quotations

The best defense against usurpatory government is an assertive citizenry.
-William F. Buckley, Jr.

The best government rests on the people and not on the few, on persons and not on property, on the free development of public opinion and not on authority.
-George Bancroft

The best leaders inspire by example. When that's not an option, brute intimidation works pretty well, too.
-Larry Kersten, PhD

The best politics for any president is to be a good president.
-Theodore H. White

The best reason I can think of for not running for President of the United States is that you have to shave twice a day.
-Adlai E. Stevenson II

The best time to listen to a politician is when he's on a stump on a street corner in the rain late at night when he's exhausted. Then he doesn't lie.
-Theodore H. White

The biases the media has are much bigger than conservative or liberal. They're about getting ratings, about making money, about doing stories that are easy to cover.
-Al Franken

The biggest and most pertinent lesson in history- at least for democracies- is that they cannot take their existence for granted.
-Norman Cousins

The broad foundation upon which our Constitution rests being the people- a breath of theirs having made, as a breath can unmake, change, or modify it- it can be assigned to none of the great divisions of government but to that of democracy.
-William Henry Harrison

The broad liberal objective is a balanced and flexible 'mixed economy,' thus seeking to occupy that middle ground between capitalism and socialism whose viability has so long been denied by both capitalists and socialists.
-Arthur Schlesinger, Jr.

The bumper sticker I'm going to have printed up for Democrats this year is, 'We're not perfect, but they're nuts.'
-Barney Frank

The career of politics grants a feeling of power. The knowledge of influencing men, of participating in power over them, and above all, the feeling of holding in one's hands a nerve fiber of historically important events can elevate the professional politician above everyday routine even when he is placed in formally modest positions.
-Max Weber

The central conservative truth is that is it culture, not politics, that determines the success of a society. The central liberal truth is that politics can change a culture and save it from itself.
-Daniel Patrick Moynihan

The challenge of politics and public service is to discover what is interfering with justice and dignity for the individual here and now, and then to decide swiftly upon the appropriate remedies.
-Robert F. Kennedy

The charade of politics is to make voters think that the personal narrative of the candidate affects the operation of the corporate state. It doesn't really matter on the fundamental issues whether the President is Republican or Democratic.
-*Chris Hedges*

The chief deduction most people make from their income tax is that government costs too darned much.
-*Walt Streightiff*

The class which has the power to rob upon a large scale has also the power to control the government and legalize their robbery.
-*Eugene V. Debs*

The common people of America display a quality of good common sense which is heartening to anyone who believes in the democratic process.
-*George Gallup*

The conservatives' preoccupation with the burning of American flags can be attributed to the amount of time they spend wrapped in them.
-*Kevin G. Barkes*

The contented and economically comfortable have a very discriminating view of government. Nobody is ever indignant about bailing out failed banks and failed savings and loans associations... But when taxes must be paid for the lower middle class and poor, the government assumes an aspect of wickedness.
-*John Kenneth Galbraith*

The conventional rules of Beltway journalism... divide the world into Democrats and Republicans, liberals and conservatives, and allow journalists to pretend they have done their job if instead of reporting the truth behind the news, they merely give each side an opportunity to spin the news.
-Bill Moyers

The convictions that leaders have formed before reaching high office are the intellectual capital they will consume as long as they continue in office. There is little time for leaders to reflect. They are locked in an endless battle in which the urgent constantly gains on the important.
-Henry Kissinger

The corporations don't have to lobby the government anymore. They are the government.
-Jim Hightower

The country was founded on the principle that the primary role of government is to protect property from the majority, and so it remains.
-Noam Chomsky

The course of history shows that as a government grows, liberty decreases.
-Thomas Jefferson

The crimes of violence committed for selfish, personal motives are historically insignificant compared to those committed ad majorem gloriam Dei, out of a self-sacrificing devotion to a flag, a leader, a religious faith or a political conviction. Man has always been prepared not only to kill but also to die for good, bad or completely futile causes. And what can be a more valid proof of the reality of the self-transcending urge than this readiness to die for an ideal?
-Arthur Koestler

The danger is not that a particular class is unfit to govern. Every class is unfit to govern. The law of liberty tends to abolish the reign of race over race, of faith over faith, of class over class.
-John Dalberg-Acton

The death of a democracy is not likely to be an assassination by ambush. It will be a slow extinction from apathy, indifference, and undernourishment.
-Robert M. Hutchins

The declining intellectual quality of political leadership is the result of the growing complexity of the world. Since no one, be he endowed with the highest wisdom, can grasp it in its entirety, it is those who are least bothered by this who strive for power.
-Stanislaw Lem

The defense of our democracy against the forces that threaten it from without has made some of its failures to function at home glaringly apparent.
-Wendell Willkie

The deterioration of a government begins almost always by the decay of its principles.
-Charles Louis de Montesquieu

The Big Book of American Political Quotations

The difference between Democrats and Republicans is: Democrats have accepted some ideas of Socialism cheerfully, while Republicans have accepted them reluctantly.
-*Norman Thomas*

The difference between a bandit and a patriot is a good press agent.
-*Will Rogers*

The difference between a democracy and a dictatorship is that in a democracy you vote first and take orders later; in a dictatorship you don't have to waste your time voting.
-*Charles Bukowski*

The difference between a politician and a statesman is: a politician thinks of the next election and a statesman thinks of the next generation.
-*James Freeman Clarke*

The difference between a prostitute and a politician is that there are some things a prostitute won't do for money.
-*Variously attributed*

The difference between a real horse race an election is that in a horse race the whole horse wins.
-*Variously attributed*

The difference between corporations and governments is governments have a monopoly on force. It's a lot easier to vote with your feet or your wallet than it is to change a government with your vote.
-*P.J. O'Rourke*

The difference between patriotism and nationalism is that the patriot is proud of his country for what it does, and the nationalist is proud of his country no matter what it does; the first attitude creates a feeling of responsibility, but the second a feeling of blind arrogance that leads to war.
-*Sydney J. Harris*

The difference between politics and baseball is that in baseball, when you get caught stealing, you're out.
-*Ron Dentinger*

The doctrine that the cure for the evils of democracy is more democracy is like saying the cure for crime is more crime.
-*H.L. Mencken*

The ear of the leader must ring with the voices of the people.
-*Woodrow Wilson*

The economic owning class is always the political ruling class.
-*Eugene V. Debs*

The effort to calculate exactly what the voters want at each particular moment leaves out of account the fact that when they are troubled the thing the voters most want is to be told what to want.
-*Walter Lippmann*

The enemy is not conservatism, the enemy is not liberalism. The enemy is bullshit.
-*Nelson Lars-Erik*

The essence of Government is power; and power, lodged as it must be in human hands, will ever be liable to abuse.
-*James Madison*

The essence of a free government consists in an effectual control of rivalries.
-John Adams

The essential humanity of men can be protected and preserved only where government must answer- not just to the wealthy, not just to those of a particular religion, or a particular race, but to all its people.
-Robert F. Kennedy

The essential ingredient of politics is timing.
-Pierre Elliott Trudeau

The evils of government are directly proportional to the tolerance of the people.
-Frank Kent

The evils we experience flow from the excess of democracy. The people do not want virtue, but are the dupes of pretended patriots. (speech at the 1787 Constitutional Convention)
-Elbridge Gerry

The existence of a free market does not of course eliminate the need for government. On the contrary, government is essential both as a forum for determining the 'rule of the game' and as an umpire to interpret and enforce the rules decided on.
-Milton Friedman

The fact that political ideologies are tangible realities is not a proof of their vitally necessary character. The bubonic plague was an extraordinarily powerful social reality, but no one would have regarded it as vitally necessary.
-Wilhelm Reich

The fact that so many successful politicians are such shameless liars is not only a reflection on them, it is also a reflection on us. When the people want the impossible, only liars can satisfy.
-*Thomas Sowell*

The final test of a leader is that he leaves behind him in other men, the conviction and the will to carry on.
-*Walter Lippmann*

The first responsibility of a leader is to define reality.
-*Max DePree*

The first thing I'll do if elected is demand a recount.
-*Kinky Friedman*

The first thing we do with a President is shunt him off to a siding where nothing American can ever happen to him.
-*Russell Baker*

The flood of money that gushes into politics today is a pollution of democracy.
-*Theodore H. White*

The founding fathers, in their wisdom, devised a method by which our republic can take one hundred of its most prominent numbskulls and keep them out of the private sector where they might do actual harm.
-*P.J. O'Rourke*

The future holds little hope for any government where the present holds no hope for the people.
-*Lyndon B. Johnson*

The general will rule in society as the private will governs each separate individual.
-*Maximilien Robespierre*

The genius of a good leader is to leave behind him a situation which common sense, without the grace of genius, can deal with successfully.
-*Walter Lippmann*

The genius of capitalism consists precisely in its lack of morality. Unless he is rich enough to hire his own choir, a capitalist is a fellow who, by definition, can ill afford to believe in anything other than the doctrine of the bottom line. Deprive a capitalist of his God-given right to lie and cheat and steal, and the poor sap stands a better than even chance of becoming one of the abominable wards of the state from whose grimy fingers the Reagan Administration hopes to snatch the ark of democracy.
-*Lewis H. Lapham*

The gentle government that promises to hold your hand as you cross the street refuses to let go on the other side.
-*Theodore Forstman*

The gentlemen who wrote the Constitution were as suspicious of efficient government as they were wary of democracy, a 'turbulence and a folly' that was associated with the unruly ignorance of an urban mob.
-*Lewis H. Lapham*

The goal in the end is not to win elections. The goal is to change society.
-*Paul Krugman*

The good news, to relieve all this gloom, is that a democracy is inherently self-correcting. Here, the people are sovereign. Inept political leaders can be replaced. Foolish policies can be changed. Disastrous mistakes can be reversed.
-Theodore (Ted) Sorensen

The government and the church are two different realms of service, and those in political office have to face a subtle but important difference between the implementation of the high ideals of religious faith and public duty.
-Jimmy Carter

The government consists of a gang of men exactly like you and me. They have, taking one with another, no special talent for the business of government; they have only a talent for getting and holding office.
-H.L. Mencken

The government deficit is the difference between the amount of money the government spends and the amount it has the nerve to collect.
-Sam Ewing

The government in a revolution is the despotism of liberty against tyranny.
-Maximilien Robespierre

The government is becoming the family of last resort.
-Jerry Brown

The government is mainly an expensive organization to regulate evil-doers and tax those who behave.
-E.W. Howe

The government is not God. It does not have the right to take away that which it can't return even if it wants to.
-Anton Chekhov

The government is not your mommy.
-Variously attributed

The government of an exclusive company of merchants is, perhaps, the worst of all governments for any country whatever.
-Adam Smith

The government that can protect you from your enemies can be used as easily by your enemies to harm you.
-Harry Browne

The government they devised was defective from the start, requiring several amendments, a civil war, and major social transformations to attain the system of constitutional government and its respect for the freedoms and individual rights, we hold as fundamental today.
-Thurgood Marshall

The government we mean to erect is intended to last for ages.
-James Madison

The government, which was designed for the people, has got into the hands of the bosses and their employers, the special interests. An invisible empire has been set up above the forms of democracy.
-Woodrow Wilson

The great difficulty with politics is, that there are no established principles.
-Napoleon Bonaparte

The great problem of legislation is, so to organize the civil government of a community... that in the operation of human institutions upon social action, self-love and social may be made the same.
-John Quincy Adams

The great thing about democracy is that it gives every voter a chance to do something stupid.
-Art Spander

The greatest blessing of our democracy is freedom. But in the last analysis, our only freedom is the freedom to discipline ourselves.
-Bernard Baruch

The hardest thing about any political campaign is how to win without proving that you are unworthy of winning.
-Adlai E. Stevenson II

The hatred Americans have for their own government is pathological, if understandable. At one level it is simply thwarted greed: since our religion is making a buck, giving a part of that buck to any government is an act against nature.
-Gore Vidal

The health of a democratic society may be measured by the quality of functions performed by private citizens.
-Alexis de Tocqueville

The heights of popularity and patriotism are still the beaten road to power and tyranny; flattery to treachery; standing armies to arbitrary government; and the glory of God to the temporal interest of the clergy.
-David Hume

The Big Book of American Political Quotations

The high sentiments always win in the end- the leaders who offer blood, toil, tears, and sweat always get more out of their followers than those who offer safety and a good time. When it comes to the pinch, human beings are heroic.
-George Orwell

The highest patriotism is not a blind acceptance of official policy, but a love of one's country deep enough to call her to a higher plane.
-George McGovern

The history of American politics is littered with bodies of people who took so pure a position that they had no clout at all.
-Ben Bradlee

The history of liberty is a history of the limitation of governmental power, not the increase of it.
-Woodrow Wilson

The idea of democracy has been stripped of its moral imperatives and come to denote hollowness and hypocrisy.
-Paul Wellstone

The idea that you can merchandise candidates for high office like breakfast cereal is the ultimate indignity to the democratic process.
-Adlai E. Stevenson II

The ideal form of government is democracy tempered with assassination.
-Voltaire (François Marie Arouet)

The ideally non-violent state will be an ordered anarchy. That State is the best governed which is governed the least.
-Mohandas K. Gandhi

The ideas of a time are like the clothes of a season: they are as arbitrary, as much imposed by some superior will which is seldom explicit. They are utilitarian and political, the instruments of smooth-running government.
-*Wyndham Lewis*

The impersonal hand of government can never replace the helping hand of a neighbor.
-*Hubert H. Humphrey*

The incestuous relationship between government and big business thrives in the dark.
-*Jack Anderson*

The income tax created more criminals than any other single act of government.
-*Barry M. Goldwater*

The insane have achieved political respectability while the sane act too good for it all. The irrational celebrate while the rational act bored and above-it-all.
-*Maureen Dowd*

The interpretation of constitutional principles must not be too literal. We must remember that the machinery of government would not work if it were not allowed a little play in its joints.
-*Oliver Wendell Holmes, Jr.*

The intoxication of power rapidly sobers off in the knowledge of its restrictions and under the prompt reminder of an ever-present and not always considerate press, as well as the kindly suggestions that not infrequently come from Congress.
-*William Howard Taft*

The Big Book of American Political Quotations

The introduction of religious passion into politics is the end of honest politics, and the introduction of politics into religion is the prostitution of true religion.
-Lord Hailsham

The issue is not that morals be applied to public policy, it's that conservatives bring public policy to spheres of our lives where it should not enter.
-Barney Frank

The issue of environmental quality is one which transcends traditional political boundaries. It is a cause which can attract, and very sincerely, liberals, conservatives, radicals, reactionaries, freaks, and middle-class straights.
-Russell Kirk

The kind of man who wants the government to adopt and enforce his ideas is always the kind of man whose ideas are idiotic.
-H.L. Mencken

The largest party in the United States is the 50 percent who don't vote.
-Susan Sarandon

The last thing a political party gives up is its vocabulary.
-Alexis de Tocqueville

The laws and the entire scheme of our civil rule, from the town meeting to the State capitals and the national capital, is yours. Your every voter, as surely as your Chief Magistrate, under the same high sanction, though in a different sphere, exercises a public trust.
-Grover Cleveland

The legislative department is everywhere extending the sphere of its activity and drawing all power into its impetuous vortex.
-*James Madison*

The lessons of paternalism ought to be unlearned and the better lesson taught that while the people should patriotically and cheerfully support their government, its functions do not include the support of the people.
-*Grover Cleveland*

The liberal left can be as rigid and destructive as any force in American life.
-*Daniel Patrick Moynihan*

The liberals can understand everything but people who don't understand them.
-*Lenny Bruce*

The man who can make others laugh secures more votes for a measure than the man who forces them to think.
-*Malcolm de Chazal*

The man who stands by and says nothing, when the peril of his government is discussed, cannot be misunderstood. If not hindered, he is sure to help the enemy.
-*Abraham Lincoln*

The manners of women are the surest criterion by which to determine whether a republican government is practicable in a nation or not.
-*John Quincy Adams*

The marvel of all history is the patience with which men and women submit to burdens unnecessarily laid upon them by their governments.
-*William H. Borah*

The methods now being used to merchandise the political candidate as though he were a deodorant positively guarantee the electorate against ever hearing the truth about anything.
-*Aldous Huxley*

The mightiest of weapons is truth. And everyone knows you're not permitted to bring a weapon into a Government building.
-*John Alejandro King (The Covert Comic)*

The military don't start wars. Politicians start wars.
-*William C. Westmoreland*

The mistakes made by Congress wouldn't be so bad if the next Congress didn't keep trying to correct them.
-*Cullen Hightower*

The modern conservative is engaged in one of man's oldest exercises in moral philosophy, that is the search for a superior moral justification for selfishness.
-*John Kenneth Galbraith*

The moral test of government is how it treats those who are in the dawn of life, the children; those who are in the twilight of life, the aged; and those in the shadows of life, the sick, the needy and the handicapped.
-*Hubert H. Humphrey*

The more you read and observe about this Politics thing, you got to admit that each party is worse than the other. The one that's out always looks the best.
-*Will Rogers*

The most dangerous moment for a bad government is when it begins to reform.
-*Alexis de Tocqueville*

The most effective means of ensuring the government's accountability to the people is an aggressive, free, challenging, untrusting press.
-*Colin Powell*

The most effective way to restrict democracy is to transfer decision-making from the public arena to unaccountable institutions: kings and princes, priestly castes, military juntas, party dictatorships, or modern corporations.
-*Noam Chomsky*

The most extravagant idea that can be born in the head of a political thinker is to believe that it suffices for people to enter, weapons in hand, among a foreign people and expect to have its laws and constitution embraced. No one loves armed missionaries; the first lesson of nature and prudence is to repulse them as enemies.
-*Maximilien Robespierre*

The most fundamental liberal failure of the current era: the failure to embrace a moral vision of America based on the transcendent faith that human beings are more than the sum of their material appetites, our country is more than an economic machine, and freedom is not license but responsibility.
-*Bill Moyers*

The most important political office is that of private citizen.
-*Louis Brandeis*

The most radical revolutionary will become a conservative the day after the revolution.
-*Hannah Arendt*

The most tyrannical of governments are those which make crimes of opinions, for everyone has an inalienable right to his thoughts.
-*Baruch Spinoza*

The most valuable function performed by the federal government is entertainment.
-*Dave Barry*

The mystery of government is not how Washington works but how to make it stop.
-*P.J. O'Rourke*

The natural progress of things is for liberty to yield and government to gain ground.
-*Thomas Jefferson*

The necessary foundation of every authoritarian government is a public that prefers to feel rather than to reason. Emotion is the wild stag skillfully ridden by all dictators.
-*Brian Ferguson*

The newspaper is in all its literalness the bible of democracy, the book out of which a people determines its conduct.
-*Walter Lippmann*

The next time they give you all that civic bullshit about voting, keep in mind that Hitler was elected in a full, free democratic election.
-George Carlin

The next time, for God's sake, let's at least do a background check before we make someone President.
-David Letterman

The nine most terrifying words in the English language are 'I'm from the government, and I'm here to help.'
-Ronald Reagan

The obligation to die must carry with it the right to live. If every citizen owes it to society that he must fight for it in case of need, then society owes to every citizen the opportunity of a livelihood. 'Unemployment,' in the case of the willing and able becomes henceforth a social crime. Every democratic Government must henceforth take as the starting point of its industrial policy, that there shall be no such thing as able bodied men and women 'out of work,' looking for occupation and unable to find it.
-Stephen Leacock

The office of President requires the constitution of an athlete, the patience of a mother, and the endurance of an early Christian.
-Woodrow Wilson

The office of government is not to confer happiness, but to give men opportunity to work out happiness for themselves.
-William Ellery Channing

The office of the president is such a bastardized thing, half royalty and half democracy, that nobody knows whether to genuflect or spit.
-Jimmy Breslin

The one pervading evil of democracy is the tyranny of the majority, or rather of that party, not always the majority, that succeeds, by force or fraud, in carrying elections.
-John Dalberg-Acton

The one thing that I know government is good for is countervailing against monopoly. It's not great at that either, but it's the only force I know that is fairly reliable.
-John Perry Barlow

The only difference I ever found between the Democratic leadership and the Republican leadership is that one of them is skinning you from the ankle up and the other, from the ear down.
-Huey P. Long

The only difference between the Democrats and the Republicans is that the Democrats allow the poor to be corrupt, too.
-Oscar Levant

The only legitimate right to govern is an express grant of power from the governed.
-William Henry Harrison

The only reason Congress isn't like a petulant child grabbing a ball and going home is an excess of petulant children and a lack of balls.
-Will Durst

The only sure bulwark of continuing liberty is a government strong enough to protect the interests of the people and a people strong enough and well enough informed to maintain its sovereign control over the government.
-Franklin Delano Roosevelt

The only test of leadership is that somebody follows.
-*Robert K. Greenleaf*

The only thing more dangerous than a politician who thinks about re-election, is a politician who doesn't think about re-election.
-*James Carville*

The only time you can believe a politician is when he says his opponent is a lying thief.
-*Will Durst*

The only way to change is to vote. People are responsible.
-*Paul Wellstone*

The only way to win an election by a greater margin than Saddam Hussein in Iraq is to be a Democratic candidate in Chicago.
-*John Alejandro King (The Covert Comic)*

The ordinary politician has a very low estimate of human nature. In his daily life he comes into contact chiefly with persons who want to get something or to avoid something. Beyond this circle of seekers after privileges, individuals and organized minorities, he is aware of a large unorganized, indifferent mass of citizens who ask nothing in particular and rarely complain. The politician comes after a while to think that the art of politics is to satisfy the seekers after favors and to mollify the inchoate mass with noble sentiments and patriotic phrases.
-*Walter Lippmann*

The organization of American society is an interlocking system of semi-monopolies notoriously venal, an electorate notoriously unenlightened, misled by a mass media notoriously phony.
-*Paul Goodman*

The Big Book of American Political Quotations

The other day, someone told me the difference between a democracy and a people's democracy. It's the same difference between a jacket and a straitjacket.
-*Ronald Reagan*

The people I have no feeling for are professional killers. But I count that man no worse than a governor who won't commute a death sentence because it's unpolitical.
-*F. Lee Bailey*

The people are not satisfied with any form of government, or statute law, until it comes up to their sense of justice; so every progressive State revises its statutes from time to time, and at each revision comes nearer to the absolute right which human nature demands.
-*Theodore Parker*

The people are the best guardians of their own rights and it is the duty of their executive to abstain from interfering in or thwarting the sacred exercise of the lawmaking functions of their government.
-*William Henry Harrison*

The people cannot delegate to government the power to do anything which would be unlawful for them to do themselves.
-*John Locke*

The people have spoken, the bastards.
-*Dick Tuck*

The people of these United States are the rightful masters of both Congresses and courts, not to overthrow the Constitution, but to overthrow the men who pervert the Constitution.
-*Abraham Lincoln*

The Big Book of American Political Quotations

The people of this country, not special interest big money, should be the source of all political power.
-*Paul Wellstone*

The point to remember is that what the government gives it must first take away.
-*John Coleman*

The political arena leaves one no alternative, one must either be a dunce or a rogue.
-*Emma Goldman*

The political machine triumphs because it is a united minority against a divided majority.
-*Will Durant*

The political spectrum isn't a line so much as a circle, and no matter which direction you head from 12 o'clock, you eventually wind up on the bottom by the hatch where the cuckoos pop out.
-*Tamara K (Indiana blogger)*

The politician is an acrobat. He keeps his balance by saying the opposite of what he does.
-*Maurice Barres*

The politician is... trained in the art of inexactitude. His words tend to be blunt or rounded, because if they have a cutting edge they may later return to wound him.
-*Edward R. Murrow*

The politicians were talking themselves red, white and blue in the face. (on campaigning)
-*Clare Boothe Luce*

The poor have sometimes objected to being governed badly; the rich have always objected to being governed at all.
-G.K. Chesterton

The poor man who takes property by force is called a thief, but the creditor who can by legislation make a debtor pay a dollar twice as large as he borrowed is lauded as the friend of a sound currency. The man who wants the people to destroy the Government is an anarchist, but the man who wants the Government to destroy the people is a patriot.
-William Jennings Bryan

The preservation of freedom is in the hands of the people themselves-not of the government.
-Margaret Chase Smith

The press is not a fourth branch of government, the press plays an essential role in 'obliging the government to control itself.' And if we do not serve in this way, the rest of the rights guaranteed by our Constitution cannot be sustained.
-Katharine Graham

The press is no substitute for institutions. It is like the beam of a searchlight that moves restlessly about, bringing one episode and then another out of darkness into vision. Men cannot do the work of the world by this light alone. They cannot govern society by episodes, incidents, and eruptions. It is only when they work by a steady light of their own, that the press, when it is turned upon them, reveals a situation intelligible enough for a popular decision.
-Walter Lippmann

The Big Book of American Political Quotations

The principle that the end justifies the means is and remains the only rule of political ethics; anything else is just a vague chatter and melts away between one's fingers.
-Arthur Koestler

The problem is that the Good Lord didn't see fit to put oil and gas reserves where there are democratic governments.
-Dick Cheney

The problem with most political institutions is that they are almost congenitally incapable of responding to a problem by saying 'I don't know'.
-Richard Fernandez

The problem with political jokes is they get elected.
-Henry Cote

The proper function of a government is to make it easy for the people to do good, and difficult for them to do evil.
-Daniel Webster

The proper role of government is exactly what John Stuart Mill said in the middle of the 19th century in *On Liberty*. The proper role of government is to prevent other people from harming an individual. Government, he said, never has any right to interfere with an individual for that individual's own good.
-Milton Friedman

The proposition, that the people are the best keepers of their own liberties, is not true; they are the worst conceivable; they are no keepers at all; they can neither judge, act, think, or will, as a political body.
-John Adams

The prudent capitalist will never adventure his capital... if there exists a state of uncertainty as to whether the Government will repeal tomorrow what it has enacted today.
-*William Henry Harrison*

The public is governed as it reasons; its own prerogative is foolish speech and that of its governors is foolish action.
-*Nicolas Chamfort*

The punishment which the wise suffer who refuse to take part in the government, is to live under the government of worse men.
-*Plato*

The real question of government versus private enterprise is argued on too philosophical and abstract a basis. Theoretically, planning may be good. But nobody has ever figured out the cause of government stupidity and until they do (and find the cure) all ideal plans will fall into quicksand.
-*Richard P. Feynman*

The real reason that we can't have the Ten Commandments in a courthouse: You cannot post 'Thou shalt not steal,' 'Thou shalt not commit adultery,' and 'Thou shalt not lie' in a building full of lawyers, judges, and politicians. It creates a hostile work environment.
-*George Carlin*

The real truth of the matter is, as you and I know, that a financial element in the larger centers has owned the Government ever since the days of Andrew Jackson...
-*Franklin Delano Roosevelt*

The reason there are so few female politicians is that it is too much trouble to put makeup on two faces.
-*Maureen Murphy*

The Big Book of American Political Quotations

The reason there are two senators for each state is so that one can be the designated driver.

-Jay Leno

The rest of the people know the condition of the country, for they live in it, but Congress has no idea what is going on in America, so the President has to tell 'em.

-Will Rogers

The rich people apparently are leaving America. They're giving up their citizenship. These great lovers of America who made their money in this country- when you ask them to pay their fair share of taxes, they're running abroad. We have 19-year-old kids who died in Iraq and Afghanistan defending this country. They went abroad. Not to escape taxes. They're working class kids who died in wars and now billionaires want to run abroad to avoid paying their fair share of taxes. What patriotism! What love of country!

-Bernie Sanders

The right of voting for representatives is the primary right by which other rights are protected. To take away this right is to reduce a man to slavery, for slavery consists in being subject to the will of another, and he that has not a vote in the election of representatives is in this case.

-Thomas Paine

The right-wing of the Republican party isn't so much a political agenda as a plea for help.

-Larry Flynt

The Big Book of American Political Quotations

The rising power of the United States in world affairs... requires, not a more compliant press, but a relentless barrage of facts and criticism... Our job in this age, as I see it, is not to serve as cheerleaders for our side in the present world struggle but to help the largest possible number of people to see the realities of the changing and convulsive world in which American policy must operate.
-*James Reston*

The sad duty of politics is to establish justice in a sinful world.
-*Reinhold Neibuhr*

The saddest life is that of a political aspirant under democracy. His failure is ignominious and his success disgraceful.
-*H.L. Mencken*

The second office in the government is honorable and easy; the first is but a splendid misery.
-*Thomas Jefferson*

The simple truth is that our businessmen do not want a government that will let business alone. They want a government they can use.
-*Albert Jay Nock*

The single most exciting thing you encounter in government is competence, because it's so rare.
-*Daniel Patrick Moynihan*

The spirit of rebellion is present in every great city, and the great task of wise government is to keep it dormant, for if it wakes it is a torrent which no dam can hold back.
-*Giovanni Casanova*

The spirit of resistance to government is so valuable on certain occasions that I wish it to be always kept alive. It will often be exercised when wrong, but better so than not to be exercised at all.
-*Thomas Jefferson*

The spiritualist and the politician are magicians, one offering diversion, the other security, in exchange for a suspension of common sense.
-*David Mamet*

The strongest continuous thread in America's political tradition is skepticism about government.
-*George F. Will*

The strongest reason for the people to retain the right to keep and bear arms is, as a last resort, to protect themselves against tyranny in government.
-*Thomas Jefferson*

The stupidity of the average man will permit the oligarch, whether economic or political, to hide his real purposes from the scrutiny of his fellows and to withdraw his activities from effective control.
-*Reinhold Neibuhr*

The subjects of every state ought to contribute towards the support of the government, as nearly as possible, in proportion to their respective abilities, that is, in proportion to the revenue which they respectively enjoy under the protection of the state.
-*Adam Smith*

The success of our popular government rests wholly upon the correct interpretation of the deliberate, intelligent, dependable popular will of America.
-*Warren G. Harding*

The supply of government exceeds demand.
-*Lewis H. Lapham*

The surface of American society is covered with a layer of democratic paint, but from time to time one can see the old aristocratic colors breaking through.
-*Alexis de Tocqueville*

The tendency of democracies is, in all things, to mediocrity.
-*James Fenimore Cooper*

The theory of democratic government is not that the will of the people is always right, but rather that normal human beings of average intelligence will, if given a chance, learn the right and best course by bitter experience.
-*W.E.B. DuBois*

The thing about Republicans is that they don't care so much about respect, but they love fear, at least in others.
-*Jane Smiley*

The thing about democracy, beloveds, is that it is not neat, orderly, or quiet. It requires a certain relish for confusion.
-*Molly Ivins*

The thing about politicians is, you have to take the smooth with the smooth.
-*Susan Hill*

The things that bother the press about a President will ultimately bother the country.
-*David Halberstam*

The threat of people acting in their own enlightened and rational self-interest strikes bureaucrats, politicians and social workers as ominous and dangerous.
-*W.G. Hill*

The trade of governing has always been monopolized by the most ignorant and the most rascally individuals of mankind.
-*Thomas Paine*

The tragedy of our day is the climate of fear in which we live, and fear breeds repression. Too often sinister threats to the bill of rights, to freedom of the mind, are concealed under the patriotic cloak, of anti-communism.
-*Adlai E. Stevenson II*

The tree of liberty must be refreshed from time to time with the blood of patriots and tyrants.
-*Thomas Jefferson*

The trouble with most conservatives is that those who have brains lack guts and those who have guts lack brains.
-*Richard M. Nixon*

The trouble with politicians debating each other is that there isn't any subject that's any of their business.
-*Robert Brault*

The trouble with radicals is that they only read radical literature, and the trouble with conservatives is that they don't read anything.
-*Thomas Nixon Carver*

The trouble with this country is that there are too many politicians who believe, with a conviction based on experience, that you can fool all of the people all of the time.
-*Franklin P. Adams*

The true American patriot is by definition skeptical of the government.
-*Sarah Vowell*

The true conservative is not at home in social struggle. He will attempt to avoid unbridgeable schism, because he knows that a stable social structure thrives not on triumphs but on reconciliations.
-*Henry Kissinger*

The two greatest obstacles to democracy in the United States are, first, the widespread delusion among the poor that we have a democracy, and second, the chronic terror among the rich, lest we get it.
-*Edward Dowling*

The two real political parties in America are the Winners and the Losers.
-*Kurt Vonnegut, Jr.*

The typical citizen drops down to a lower level of mental performance as soon as he enters the political field. He argues and analyzes in a way which he would readily recognize as infantile within the sphere of his real interests. He becomes primitive again.
-*Joseph A. Schumpeter*

The tyrant scorns love; he is content with fear. If he seeks to win the love of his subjects, it is for political reasons; and if he finds a more economical way to enslave them, he adopts it immediately.
-*Jean-Paul Sartre*

The Big Book of American Political Quotations

The U.S. Constitution and the Bible have a lot in common. Few people have read them in their entirety; they are quoted out of context and cherry-picked; their official interpreters wear robes and issue pronouncements that sometimes benefit an entitled few or discriminate against women and minorities; and their decrees and commandments are simply ignored when they interfere with the interests of those in power.
-*Kevin G. Barkes*

The ultimate failures of dictatorship cost humanity far more than any temporary failures of democracy.
-*Franklin Delano Roosevelt*

The ultimate tendency of liberalism is vegetarianism.
-*Norman Mailer*

The universe is not rich enough to buy the vote of an honest man.
-*Dick Gregory*

The use of force alone is but temporary. It may subdue for a moment; but it does not remove the necessity of subduing again: and a nation is not governed, which is perpetually to be conquered.
-*Edmund Burke*

The vanquished know war. They see through the empty jingoism of those who use the abstract words of glory, honor, and patriotism to mask the cries of the wounded, the senseless killing, war profiteering, and chest-pounding grief.
-*Chris Hedges*

The very essence of a free government consists in considering offices as public trusts, bestowed for the good of the country, and not for the benefit of an individual or a party.
-*John C. Calhoun*

The very existence of government at all, infers inequality. The citizen who is preferred to office becomes the superior to those who are not, so long as he is the repository of power, and the child inherits the wealth of the parent as a controlling law of society.
-*James Fenimore Cooper*

The votes elected officials make should be based on the best interests of the American people, not the fear of retribution when shadowy groups spend millions of dollars on negative advertisements.
-*Bernie Sanders*

The way people in democracies think of the government as something different from themselves is a real handicap. And, of course, sometimes the government confirms their opinion.
-*Lewis Mumford*

The way you solve things is by making it politically profitable for the wrong people to do the right thing.
-*Milton Friedman*

The weather is like the government- always in the wrong.
-*Jerome K. Jerome*

The whole aim of practical politics is to keep the populace alarmed (and hence clamorous to be led to safety) by menacing it with an endless series of hobgoblins, all of them imaginary.
-*H.L. Mencken*

The whole dream of democracy is to raise the proletarian to the level of stupidity attained by the bourgeois.
-*Gustave Flaubert*

The Big Book of American Political Quotations

The whole idea of our government is this: if enough people get together and act in concert, they can take something and not pay for it.
-*P.J. O'Rourke*

The whole modern world has divided itself into Conservatives and Progressives. The business of Progressives is to go on making mistakes. The business of the Conservatives is to prevent the mistakes from being corrected.
- *G.K. Chesterton*

The word 'politics' is derived from the word 'poly,' meaning 'many,' and the word 'ticks,' meaning 'blood sucking parasites.'
-*Larry Hardiman*

The word 'security' is a broad, vague generality whose contours should not be invoked to abrogate the fundamental law embodied in the First Amendment. The guarding of military and diplomatic secrets at the expense of informed representative government provides no real security...
-*Hugo Black*

The word bipartisan means some larger-than-usual deception is being carried out.
-*George Carlin*

The world is a fine place. The only thing wrong with it is us. How little justice and humility there is in us, how poorly we understand patriotism!
-*Anton Chekhov*

The world is governed by far different personages than what is imagined by those not behind the scenes.
-*Benjamin Disraeli*

The world is governed more by appearances than realities, so that it is fully as necessary to seem to know something as to know it.
-Daniel Webster

The world is not going to be saved by legislation.
-William Howard Taft

The world is weary of statesmen whom democracy has degraded into politicians.
-Benjamin Disraeli

The world needs leaders of vision instead of leaders on television.
-Lech Walesa

The world of politics is always twenty years behind the world of thought.
-John Jay Chapman

The world would be a better place if people stopped voting for folksy candidates they could have a beer with and started voting for people smarter than they are.
-Marcus Sakey

The worst government is the most moral. One composed of cynics is often very tolerant and humane. But when fanatics are on top there is no limit to oppression.
-H.L. Mencken

The worst that can happen under monarchy is rule by a single imbecile, but democracy often means the rule by an assembly of three or four hundred imbeciles.
-Robert Anton Wilson

The worst thing in the world, next to anarchy, is government.
-Henry Ward Beecher

There are always too many Democratic congressmen, too many Republican congressmen, and never enough U.S. congressmen.
-Variously attributed

There are basically two kinds of conservatives, those who don't got it and blame liberals and minorities for it, and those who got it and only care about keeping it that way.
-Rack Jite

There are corrupting influences on religion and politics, and those who practice them in the name of religion or in the name of the Republican Party or in the name of America shame our faith, our party, and our country.
-John McCain

There are few things more amusing in the world of politics than watching moderate Republicans charging to the right in pursuit of greater glory.
-Mario Cuomo

There are just two rules of governance in a free society: Mind your own business. Keep your hands to yourself.
-P.J. O'Rourke

There are men in all ages who mean to govern well, but they mean to govern. They promise to be good masters, but they mean to be masters.
-Daniel Webster

There are no accidents in politics.
-Joseph P. Kennedy, Sr.

There are no friends at cards or world politics.
-*Finley Peter Dunne*

There are no liberals behind steering wheels.
-*Russell Baker*

There are no moderate Republicans left, with the exception of a few who would vote with us when it doesn't make any difference. It's the most rigid ideological party since before the Civil War.
-*Barney Frank*

There are no true friends in politics. We are all sharks circling, and waiting, for traces of blood to appear in the water.
-*Alan Clark*

There are people in Congress I would not trust to look after my plants.
-*Andy Borowitz*

There are people in government who don't want other people to know what they know. It's just another example of elitism. And I spit on elitism. Show me an elitist, and I'll show you a loser.
-*Tom Clancy*

There are severe limits to the good that the government can do for the economy, but there are almost no limits to the harm it can do.
-*Milton Friedman*

There are those who believe that, if you will only legislate to make the well-to-do prosperous, their prosperity will leak through on those below. The Democratic idea, however, has been that if you legislate to make the masses prosperous, their prosperity will find its way up through every class which rests up on them.
-*William Jennings Bryan*

There are three kinds of patriots, two bad, one good. The bad ones are the uncritical lovers and the loveless critics. Good patriots carry on a lover's quarrel with their country, a reflection of God's lover's quarrel with all the world.
-*William Sloane Coffin, Jr.*

There are times in politics when you must be on the right side and lose.
-*John Kenneth Galbraith*

There are times when even the most potent governor must wink at transgression, in order to preserve the laws inviolate for the future.
-*Herman Melville*

There are twenty-seven specific complaints against the British Crown set forth in the Declaration of Independence. To modern ears they still sound reasonable...in large part, because so many of them can be leveled against the federal government of the United States.
-*P.J. O'Rourke*

There are two fundamental problems in American politics. The first is that most Americans do not believe that elected officials represent their interests. The second is that they are correct.
-*John Gastil*

There are two things which a democratic people will always find very difficult- to begin a war and to end it.
-*Alexis de Tocqueville*

There are worse things than losing an election; the worst thing is to lose one's convictions and not tell the people the truth.
-*Adlai E. Stevenson II*

There can be no bosses in our country except the people. The job of the government is to serve, not to dominate.
-Henry Ford

There can be no greater error than to expect or calculate upon real favors from nation to nation.
-George Washington

There can be no wise politics without thought beforehand.
-Annie Besant

There comes a time in every campaign when even a candidate you admire becomes your worst enemy.
-George Stephanopoulos

There has never been a perfect government, because men have passions; and if they did not have passions, there would be no need for government.
-Voltaire (François Marie Arouet)

There is a cult of ignorance in the United States, and there always has been. The strain of anti-intellectualism has been a constant thread winding its way through our political and cultural life, nurtured by the false notion that democracy means that 'my ignorance is just as good as your knowledge.'
-Isaac Asimov

There is a higher law than the law of government. That's the law of conscience.
-Stokely Carmichael

There is a tragic flaw in our precious Constitution, and I don't know what can be done to fix it. This is it: Only nut cases want to be president.
-*Kurt Vonnegut, Jr.*

There is always some basic principle that will ultimately get the Republican party together. If my observations are worth anything, that basic principle is the cohesive power of public plunder.
-*A.J. McLaurin*

There is an elegant memorial in Washington to Jefferson, but none to Hamilton. However, if you seek Hamilton's monument, look around. You are living in it. We honor Jefferson, but live in Hamilton's country, a mighty industrial nation with a strong central government.
-*George F. Will*

There is but one unconditional commandment, which is that we should seek incessantly, with fear and trembling, so to vote and to act as to bring about the very largest total universe of good which we can see.
-*William James*

There is but one way for a newspaperman to look at a politician and that is down.
-*Frank H. Simonds*

There is danger from all men. The only maxim of a free government ought to be to trust no man living with power to endanger the public liberty.
-*John Adams*

There is danger in reckless change, but greater danger in blind conservatism.
-*Henry George*

There is more selfishness and less principle among members of Congress, as well as others, than I had any conception (of), before I became President of the U.S.
-James K. Polk

There is no Constitutional issue here. The command of the Constitution is plain. There is no moral issue. It is wrong- deadly wrong- to deny any of your fellow Americans the right to vote in this country. There is no issue of States' rights or National rights. There is only the struggle for human rights.
-Lyndon B. Johnson

There is no Democratic or Republican way of cleaning the streets.
-Fiorello LaGuardia

There is no act of treachery or meanness of which a political party is not capable; for in politics there is no honor.
-Benjamin Disraeli

There is no art which one government sooner learns of another than that of draining money from the pockets of the people.
-Adam Smith

There is no distinctly American criminal class- except Congress.
-Mark Twain

There is no excitement anywhere in the world, short of war, to match the excitement of the American presidential campaign.
-Theodore H. White

There is no hope even that woman, with her right to vote, will ever purify politics.
-Emma Goldman

The Big Book of American Political Quotations

There is no kind of dishonesty into which otherwise good people more easily and frequently fall than that of defrauding the government.
-Benjamin Franklin

There is no more dangerous thing for a democracy than a foreign policy based on presidential preventive war.
-Arthur Schlesinger, Jr.

There is no nation on earth powerful enough to accomplish our overthrow. Our destruction, should it come at all, will be from another quarter. From the inattention of the people to the concerns of their government, from their carelessness and negligence.
-Daniel Webster

There is no nonsense so arrant that it cannot be made the creed of the vast majority by adequate governmental action.
-Bertrand Russell

There is no place for government to prohibit consumers from buying products the effect of which will be to harm themselves.
-Milton Friedman

There is no private domain of a person's life that is not political, and there is no political issue that is not ultimately personal.
-Charlotte Bunch

There is no right in the world not to be offended. That right simply doesn't exist. In a free society, an open society, people have strong opinions, and these opinions very often clash. In a democracy, we have to learn to deal with this.
-Salman Rushdie

The Big Book of American Political Quotations

There is no slippery slope toward loss of liberty, only a long staircase where each step down must first be tolerated by the American people and their leaders.
-Alan Simpson

There is not such a cradle of democracy upon the earth as the Free Public Library, this republic of letters, where neither rank, office, nor wealth receives the slightest consideration.
-Andrew Carnegie

There is nothing I dread so much as a division of the Republic into two great parties, each arranged under its leader and converting measures in opposition to each other. This, in my humble apprehension, is to be dreaded as the greatest political evil under our Constitution.
-John Adams

There is one expanding horror in American life. It is that our long odyssey toward liberty, democracy and freedom-for-all may be achieved in such a way that utopia remains forever closed, and we live in freedom and hell, debased of style, not individual from one another, void of courage, our fear rationalized away.
-Norman Mailer

There is one solution to all of our problems: Teaching our kids clarity of thought and political representation in democracy. That's it.
-Richard Dreyfuss

There is only one thing more harmful to society than an elected official forgetting the promises he made in order to get elected; that's when he doesn't forget them.
-John McCarthy

There is something inherently wrong, something out of accord with the ideals of representative democracy, when one portion of our citizenship turns its activities to private gain amid defensive war while another is fighting, sacrificing, or dying for national preservation.
-Warren G. Harding

There may be two libertarians somewhere who agree with one another, but I am not one of them.
-David Friedman

There remains still in the people a supreme power to remove or alter the legislative, when they find the legislative act contrary to the trust reposed in them.
-John Locke

There will always be leaks; in Washington, everywhere.
-Ben Bradlee

There's a true schizophrenia where if you say to voters, you know, do you think the federal government spends too much money and they should spend less, they say yeah, absolutely. Then you name specific things, like Pell grants for students and they say, no, not that. How 'bout NIH, medical research funding? Nah, you really shouldn't cut that. And pretty soon you've proved that what the American public is against is arithmetic.
-Bill Gates

There's a whole argument in the relief world about whether aid undermines the social and political contract between the state and its citizens. But if the government can't provide assistance, do you want to allow people to die?
-Paul Harvey

There's just one rule for politicians all over the world: Don't say in Power what you say in Opposition; if you do, you only have to carry out what the other fellows have found impossible.
-John Galsworthy

There's no one more intolerant than a liberal in San Francisco.
-Tim Goodman

There's no trick to being a humorist when you have the whole government working for you.
-Will Rogers

There's no way to rule innocent men. The only power any government has is the power to crack down on criminals. Well, when there aren't enough criminals, one makes them. One declares so many things to be a crime that it becomes impossible to live without breaking laws.
-Ayn Rand

These are the times that try men's souls. The summer soldier and the sunshine patriot will, in this crisis, shrink from the service of their country; but he that stands it now deserves the love and thanks of man and woman.
-Thomas Paine

These days many politicians are demanding change. Just like homeless people.
-George Carlin

These manly sentiments, in private life, make good citizens; in public life, the patriot and the hero.
-James Otis, Jr.

They (who) seek to establish systems of government based on the regimentation of all human beings by a handful of individual rulers... call this a new order. It is not new and it is not order.
-*Franklin Delano Roosevelt*

They always throw around this term 'the liberal elite.' And I kept thinking to myself about the Christian right. What's more elite than believing that only you will go to heaven?
-*Jon Stewart*

They don't want you to vote. If they did, we wouldn't vote on a Tuesday. In November. You ever throw a party on a Tuesday? No. Because nobody would come.
-*Chris Rock*

They go up there and forget who brung 'em to the dance. (re: Congressmen in Washington, DC)
-*Ann Richards*

They offer me neither food nor drink- intellectual nor spiritual consolation... (Conservatism) leads nowhere; it satisfies no ideal; it conforms to no intellectual standard, it is not safe, or calculated to preserve from the spoilers that degree of civilization which we have already attained.
-*John Maynard Keynes*

They pick a President and then for four years they pick on him.
-*Adlai E. Stevenson II*

They say that women talk too much. If you have worked in Congress you know that the filibuster was invented by men.
-*Clare Boothe Luce*

They tell us that we live in a great free republic; that our institutions are democratic; that we are a free and self-governing people. That is too much, even for a joke.
-Eugene V. Debs

They'd (politicians) do the right thing, if they thought they could get away with it.
-A. Ernst Fitzgerald

Things get very lonely in Washington sometimes. The real voice of the great people of America sometimes sounds faint, and sometimes sounds distant in that strange city. You hear politics until you wish that both parties were smothered in their own gas.
-Woodrow Wilson

Things on the whole are much faster in America; people don't 'stand for election', they 'run for office.'
-Jessica Mitford

Think of the press as a great keyboard on which the government can play.
-Joseph Goebbels

This always confuses liberals, that conservatives like the military and don't like the bureaucracy. That's because the military has their guns pointed out and the bureaucracy has them pointed in.
-Grover Norquist

This campaign not only hears the voices of the entrepreneurs and the farmers and the entrepreneurs, we hear the voices of those struggling to get ahead.
-George W. Bush

This concept of 'national defense' cannot be deemed an end in itself, justifying any exercise of legislative power designed to promote such a goal.
-*Earl Warren*

This country has come to feel the same when Congress is in session as when the baby gets hold of a hammer.
-*Will Rogers*

This country has gotten where it is in spite of politics, not by the aid of it. That we have carried as much political bunk as we have and still survived shows we are a super nation.
-*Will Rogers*

This country, with its institutions, belongs to the people who inhabit it. Whenever they shall grow weary of the existing Government, they can exercise their constitutional right of amending it or their revolutionary right to dismember or overthrow it.
-*Abraham Lincoln*

This is a government of the people, by the people and for the people no longer. It is a government of corporations, by corporations, and for corporations.
-*Rutherford B. Hayes*

This is not an easy time for humorists because the government is far funnier than we are.
-*Art Buchwald*

This is one of the paradoxes of the democratic movement- that it loves a crowd and fears the individuals who compose it- that the religion of humanity should have no faith in human beings.
-*Walter Lippmann*

This is quite a game, politics. There are no permanent enemies, and no permanent friends, only permanent interests.
-*William Clay*

This is the time for truth, not falsehood. In a Democratic nation, no one likes to say that his inspiration came from secret arrangements by closed doors, but in the sense that is how my candidacy began. I am here as your candidate tonight in large part because during four administrations of both parties, a terrible war has been chartered behind closed doors.
-*George McGovern*

Those advocates who work for world peace by urging a system of world government are called impractical dreamers. Those impractical dreamers are entitled to ask their critics what is so practical about war.
-*Walter Cronkite*

Those against politics are in favor of the politics inflicted upon them.
-*Bertolt Brecht*

Those people who treat politics and morality separately will never understand either of them.
-*Jean Jacques Rousseau*

Those who cannot think or take responsibility for themselves need, and clamor for, a leader.
-*Hermann Hesse*

Those who won our independence by revolution were not cowards. They did not fear political change. They did not exalt order at the cost of liberty. To courageous, self-reliant men, with confidence in the power of free and fearless reasoning applied through the processes of popular government, no danger flowing from speech can be deemed clear and present, unless the incidence of the evil apprehended is so imminent that it may befall before there is opportunity for full discussion. If there be time to expose through discussion the falsehood and fallacies, to avert the evil by the processes of education, the remedy to be applied is more speech, not enforced silence.
-Louis Brandeis

Though the people support the government, the government should not support the people.
-Grover Cleveland

Three groups spend other people's money: children, thieves, politicians. All three need supervision.
-Dick Armey

To acquire immunity to eloquence is of the utmost importance to the citizens of a democracy.
-Bertrand Russell

To declare that in the administration of the criminal law the end justifies the means- to declare that the government may commit crimes in order to secure the conviction of a private criminal- would bring terrible retribution.
-Louis Brandeis

The Big Book of American Political Quotations

To deny political equality is to rob the ostracized of all self-respect; of credit in the market place; of recompense in the world of work; of a voice among those who make and administer the law; a choice in the jury before whom they are tried, and in the judge who decides their punishment.
-*Elizabeth Cady Stanton*

To do evil that good may come of it is for bunglers in politics as well as morals.
-*William Penn*

To err is human. To blame someone else is politics.
-*Hubert H. Humphrey*

To expect the government to save you is to be a bystander in your own fate.
-*Mark Steyn*

To govern men, you must either excel them in their accomplishments, or despise them.
-*Benjamin Disraeli*

To listen to the interests of all, marks an ordinary government; to foresee them, marks a great government.
-*Napoleon Bonaparte*

To make democracy work, we must be a notion of participants, not simply observers. One who does not vote has no right to complain.
-*Louis L'Amour*

The Big Book of American Political Quotations

To mix environmental concerns with the frantic fantasies that people have about one political party or another is to miss the cold truth- that there is very little difference between the parties, except a difference in pandering rhetoric.
-*Michael Crichton*

To produce the desirable changes, as early as may be expedient, may therefore require the incitement and patronage of government.
-*Alexander Hamilton*

To strike freedom of the mind with the fist of patriotism is an old an ugly subtlety.
-*Adlai E. Stevenson II*

To the efficacy and permanency of your Union, a Government for the whole is indispensable.
-*George Washington*

To the victor belongs the responsibility of good government.
-*Fiorello LaGuardia*

Today most Americans seem to have forgotten the ancient evils which forced their ancestors to flee to this new country and to form a government stripped of old powers used to oppress them.
-*Hugo Black*

Tolerance is an admirable intellectual gift, but it is worth little in politics.
-*Woodrow Wilson*

Too many critics mistake the deliberations of the Congress for its decisions.
-*Sam Rayburn*

Too often in politics, there are fallacious either/or arguments put up as a justification or an excuse for an action or view which is skewed in such a way as too suggest that there is only one acceptable choice.
-*Peter Garrett*

Totalitarianism is patriotism institutionalized.
-*Steve Allen*

Tradition means giving votes to the most obscure of all classes, our ancestors. It is the democracy of the dead.
-*G.K. Chesterton*

Trial by jury. Live wherever you can make a living. How could a government based on such principles fail?
-*Stephen Ambrose*

Trickery is what humans are all about. They're so keen on tricking one another all the time that they elect governments to do it for them.
-*Terry Pratchett*

True Americanism is opposed utterly to any political divisions resting on race and religion.
-*Henry Cabot Lodge*

True Patriotism, it seems to me, is based on tolerance and a large measure of humility.
-*Adlai E. Stevenson II*

True democracy makes no enquiry about the color of skin, or the place of nativity, wherever it sees man, it recognizes a being endowed by his Creator with original inalienable rights.
-*Salmon P. Chase*

The Big Book of American Political Quotations

True patriotism hates injustice in its own land more than anywhere else.
-*Clarence Darrow*

True republicanism is the sovereignty of the people. There are natural and imprescriptible rights which an entire nation has no right to violate.
-*Marquis de Lafayette*

Trust cannot be bought or commanded, inherited or enforced. To maintain it, leaders must continually earn it.
-*Max DePree*

Trust nothing to the enthusiasm of the people. Give them a strong and a just, and, if possible, a good, government; but, above all, a strong one.
-*Arthur Wellesley*

Truth is a habit of integrity, not a strategy of politics.
-*George McGovern*

Truth is not determined by majority vote.
-*Doug Gwyn*

Truth is the glue that holds government together. Compromise is the oil that makes governments go.
-*Gerald R. Ford*

Truth no longer matters in the context of politics and, sadly, in the context of cable news.
-*Aaron Brown*

Trying to take money out of politics is like trying to take jumping out of basketball.
-*Bill Bradley*

Two Cheers for Democracy: one because it admits variety and two because it permits criticism. Two cheers are quite enough: there is no occasion to give three.
-*E.M. Forster*

Two characteristics of government are that it cannot do anything quickly, and that it never knows when to quit.
-*George Stigler*

Two hundred years ago, our Founding Fathers gave us a democracy. It was based upon the simple, yet noble, idea that government derives its validity from the consent of the governed.
-*Paul Tsongas*

Two hundred years ago, we had Jefferson, Washington, Ben Franklin and Tom Paine, and there were four million people. Today we have 220 million, and look at our leaders. Darwin was wrong.
-*Mort Sahl*

Two roads diverged in the Old Senate Office Building and I took the one less recommended, and that has made all the difference. The truth is more prosaic: I wanted a good job.
-*Theodore (Ted) Sorensen*

Ultimately all the questions boil down to one- Whether we as a people will try fearfully and futilely to preserve democracy by adopting totalitarian methods, or whether in accordance with our traditions, and our constitution we will have the confidence and courage to be free.
-*Hugo Black*

Umpires would be natural Republicans- dead to human feelings.
-*George F. Will*

Under current law, it is a crime for a private citizen to lie to a government official, but not for the government official to lie to the people.
-*Donald M. Fraser*

Under democracy, one party always devotes its chief energies to trying to prove that the other party is unfit to rule- and both commonly succeed, and are right.
-*H.L. Mencken*

Under every stone lurks a politician.
-*Aristophanes*

Under the influence of politicians, masses of people tend to ascribe the responsibility for wars to those who wield power at any given time... This is passing the buck.
-*Wilhelm Reich*

Unemployment more than anything else made me politically conscious.
-*Harold Wilson*

Unfortunately, you can't vote the rascals out, because you never voted them in, in the first place.
-*Noam Chomsky*

Unless democracy is to commit suicide by consenting to its own destruction, it will have to find some formidable answer to those who come to it saying: 'I demand from you in the name of your principles the rights which I shall deny to you later in the name of my principles.'
-*Walter Lippmann*

Unless education promotes character making, unless it helps men to be more moral, more just to their fellows, more law abiding, more discriminatingly patriotic and public spirited, it is not worth the trouble taken to furnish it.

-William Howard Taft

Unless people like you give us a new generation, willing to take on the challenge of self-government, willing to accept its responsibilities, to reform it, to change it, to make it fairer and more responsive-unless you do, the very rich will get richer, the poor will become fired in their desperation, violence will increase and here, as in so many places around the world, the purpose of government will be reduced basically to a matter of maintaining order instead of improving conditions.

-Mario Cuomo

Unless your government is respectable, foreigners will invade your rights; and to maintain tranquility you must be respectable; even to observe neutrality you must have a strong government.

-Alexander Hamilton

Unlike liberalism, with its fundamental belief in the long-range power of ideas, conservatism is bound by the stock of ideas inherited at a given time. And since it does not really believe in the power of argument, its last resort is generally a claim to superior wisdom, based on some self-arrogated superior quality.

-Friedrich Hayek

Unlike presidential administrations, problems rarely have terminal dates.

-Dwight D. Eisenhower

Until politics are a branch of science we shall do well to regard political and social reforms as experiments rather than short-cuts to the millennium.
-J.B.S. Haldane

Usually an elected official who has compromised to get nominated, compromised to get elected, and compromised repeatedly to stay in office.
-Dick Gregory

Violence has no constitutional sanction; and every government from the beginning has moved against it. But where grievances pile high and most of the elected spokesmen represent the Establishment, violence may be the only effective response.
-William O. Douglas

Vote for the man who promises least; he'll be the least disappointing.
-Bernard Baruch

Vote, n. The instrument and symbol of a freeman's power to make a fool of himself and a wreck of his country.
-Ambrose Bierce

Voters don't decide issues, they decide who will decide issues.
-George F. Will

Voters inclined to loathe and fear elite Ivy League schools rarely make fine distinctions between Yale and Harvard. All they know is that both are full of rich, fancy, stuck-up and possibly dangerous intellectuals who never sit down to supper in their undershirt no matter how hot the weather gets.
-Russell Baker

Voters quickly forget what a man says.
-*Richard M. Nixon*

Voting is like driving... you choose 'D' to move forwards and 'R' to go backwards.
-*Variously attributed*

War is always about betrayal, betrayal of the young by the old, of idealists by cynics, and of troops by politicians.
-*Chris Hedges*

War is destructive. The idea that you can do something constructive with war is becoming this facile, dangerous, intellectually lax political interpretation of military counter-insurgency theory.
-*Rachel Maddow*

War is just one more big government program.
-*Joseph Sobran*

War is no longer made by simply analyzed economic forces if it ever was. War is made or planned now by individual men, demagogues and dictators who play on the patriotism of their people to mislead them into a belief in the great fallacy of war when all their vaunted reforms have failed to satisfy the people they misrule.
-*Ernest Hemingway*

War is not about flag-waving and patriotism. War is about killing and death.
-*Chris Hedges*

War is nothing more than the continuation of politics by other means.
-*Karl von Clausewitz*

Wars and elections are both too big and too small to matter in the long run.
-*Brendan Gill*

Wars are fought by teenagers, you realize that. They really ought to be fought by the politicians and old people who start these wars.
-*James Clavell*

Washington, DC is a city filled with people who think they are important.
-*David Brinkley*

Washington is a city of southern efficiency and northern charm.
-*John F. Kennedy*

Washington is a place where people have always been suspect of style and overt sexuality. Too much preening signals that you're not up late studying cap-and-trade agreements.
-*Maureen Dowd*

Washington is a steering wheel that's not connected to an engine.
-*Richard Goodwin*

Washington is an endless series of mock palaces clearly built for clerks.
-*Ada Louise Huxtable*

Washington is no place for a good actor. The competition from bad actors is too great.
-*Fred Allen*

Washington is not America. It has become an alien city-state that rules America, and much of the rest of the world, in the way that Rome ruled the Roman Empire.
-Richard Maybury

Washington is the one place where you can't take friendship personally.
--Tony Snow (2007; White House Press Secretary)

Washington knows that it is not safe to kick people who are down until you find out what their next stop will be.
-Judith Martin

Washington, DC is 12 square miles bordered by reality.
-Andrew Johnson

Washington, DC is to lying what Wisconsin is to cheese.
-Dennis Miller

Watching Republicans in Washington is like watching lemmings, if lemmings jumped into cesspools instead of off cliffs.
-P.J. O'Rourke

Watergate left Washington a city ravaged by honesty.
-Russell Baker

Way down deep the American people are afraid of an entangling relationship between formal religions- or whole bodies of religious belief- and government. Apart from constitutional law and religious doctrine, there is a sense that tells us it's wrong to presume to speak for God or to claim God's sanction of our particular legislation and His rejection of all other positions. Most of us are offended when we see religion being trivialized by its appearance in political throwaway pamphlets.
-Mario Cuomo

We Americans are the ultimate innocents. We are forever desperate to believe that this time the government is telling the truth.
-Sydney Schanberg

We already know the winners of the next election. They'll be old white men who don't care about you or your problems.
-Craig Kilborn

We are a government of laws. Any laws some government hack can find to louse up a man who's down.
-Murray Kempton

We are all imperfect. We cannot expect perfect government.
-William Howard Taft

We are an age without leaders. We stopped having leaders at the end of the 20th century.
-Oriana Fallaci

We are at the point where the integrity of the individual counts and not what the political leadership or the religious leadership says to do.
-Buckminster Fuller

We are going to lose 51 states. Puerto Rico will demand statehood just for the chance not to vote for this guy.
-James Lileks

We are in a strange period of history in which a revolutionary has to be a patriot and a patriot has to be a revolutionary.
-George Orwell

We are not educated well enough to perform the necessary act of intelligently selecting our leaders.
-Walter Cronkite

We are under a Constitution, but the Constitution is what the judges say it is, and the judiciary is the safeguard of our liberty and of our property under the Constitution.
-Charles Evans Hughes

We assert the province of government to be to secure the people in the enjoyment of their unalienable rights. We throw to the winds the old dogma that governments can give rights.
-Susan B. Anthony

We believe in a government strong enough to use words like 'love' and 'compassion' and smart enough to convert our noblest aspirations into practical realities.
-Mario Cuomo

We believe in encouraging the talented, but we believe that while survival of the fittest may be a good working description of the process of evolution, a government of humans should elevate itself to a higher order.
-Mario Cuomo

We believe in only the government we need, but we insist on all the government we need.
-*Mario Cuomo*

We can and must move U.S. politics forward by means of committed participation.
-*Paul Wellstone*

We can state with conviction, therefore, that a man's support for absolute government is in direct proportion to the contempt he feels for his country.
-*Alexis de Tocqueville*

We cannot abdicate our conscience to an organization, nor to a government. 'Am I my brother's keeper?' Most certainly I am! I cannot escape my responsibility by saying the State will do all that is necessary.
-*Albert Schweitzer*

We cannot improve on the system of government handed down to us by the founders of the Republic, but we can find new ways to implement that system and realize our destiny.
-*Barbara Jordan*

We don't go into journalism to be popular. It is our job to seek the truth and put constant pressure on our leaders until we get answers.
-*Helen Thomas*

We elect Democrats to the Congress to give us stuff and we elect Republicans to the White House so we don't have to pay for it.
-*Charlie McDowell*

We have a besetting sin today in our politics where people think that you show your depth of commitment to a cause by rigidity, not just by rigidity, but impugning the motives of those on your side who try to get something done.
-Barney Frank

We have a government of too many people, by too many people, for too many people.
-Saul Pett

We have democratized elitism in this country. Now everybody can be a snob.
-David Brooks

We have the power to do any damn fool thing we want to do, and we seem to do it about every ten minutes.
- J. William Fulbright

We have two Governments in Washington: one run by the elected people- which is a minor part- and one run by the moneyed interests, which control everything.
-Studs Terkel

We have, on the whole, more liberty and less equality than Russia has. Russia has less liberty and more equality. Whether democracy should be defined primarily in terms of liberty or equality is a source of unending debate.
-Reinhold Neibuhr

We in America do not have government by the majority. We have government by the majority who participate.
-Thomas Jefferson

The Big Book of American Political Quotations

We in the press have a special role since there is no other institution in our society that can hold the President accountable. I do believe that our democracy can endure and prevail only if the American people are informed.
-*Helen Thomas*

We know full well the faults of our democracy- the handicaps of freedom- the inconvenience of dissent. But I know of no American who would not rather be a servant in the imperfect house of Freedom, than be a master of all the empires of tyranny.
-*Robert F. Kennedy*

We know now that Government by organized money is just as dangerous as Government by organized mob.
-*Franklin Delano Roosevelt*

We know that the price of seeking to force our beliefs on others is that they might someday force theirs on us. This freedom is the fundamental strength of our unique experiment in government. In the complex interplay of forces and considerations that go into the making of our laws and policies, its preservation must be a pervasive and dominant concern.
-*Mario Cuomo*

We live in a country where voting rights get gutted but *Sharknado* gets a sequel.
-*John Fugelsang*

We live in a stage of politics, where legislators seem to regard the passage of laws as much more important than the results of their enforcement.
-*William Howard Taft*

We live in a world in which politics has replaced philosophy.
-Martin L. Gross

We live under a government of men and morning newspapers.
-Wendell Phillips

We live under a republican form of government. We need forever to remember that representative government does represent. A careless, indifferent representative is the result of a careless, indifferent electorate. The people who start to elect a man to get what he can for his district will probably find they have elected a man who will get what he can for himself.
-Calvin Coolidge

We love America just as much as they do. But in a different way. You see, they love America like a four-year-old loves his mommy. Liberals love America like grown-ups. To a four-year-old, everything Mommy does is wonderful and anyone who criticizes Mommy is bad. Grown-up love means actually understanding what you love, taking the good with the bad and helping your loved one grow. Love takes attention and work and is the best thing in the world.
-Al Franken

We may not imagine how our lives could be more frustrating and complex- but Congress can.
-Cullen Hightower

We mistake politics for legislative debate. You can be passionate without being personal.
-Richard Dreyfuss

We must all obey the great law of change. It is the most powerful law of nature, and the means perhaps of its conservation.
-Edmund Burke

We must face the fact that the United States is neither omnipotent nor omniscient- that we are only six percent of the world's population- that we cannot impose our will upon the other 94 percent of mankind- that we cannot right every wrong or reverse each adversity- and that therefore there cannot be an American solution to every world problem. -Theodore (Ted) Sorensen

We must judge of a form of government by it's general tendency, not by happy accidents.
-Thomas Babington Macaulay

We must make our choice. We may have democracy, or we may have wealth concentrated in the hands of a few, but we can't have both.
-Louis Brandeis

We must recognize the full human equality of all of our people before God, before the law, and in the councils of government. We must do this, not because it is economically advantageous, although it is; not because the laws of God command it, although they do; not because people in other lands wish it so. We must do it for the single and fundamental reason that it is the right thing to do.
-Robert F. Kennedy

We must smother the internal and external enemies of the Republic or perish with it; now in this situation, the first maxim of your policy ought to be to lead the people by reason and the people's enemies by terror.
-Maximilien Robespierre

We need a president who's fluent in at least one language.
-Buck Henry

We need conservatives that can accept gays, and then we need hippies that can shave and bathe.
-*Patton Oswalt*

We need to ask our policy makers and those we elect to office who are supposed to make decisions to give us the evidence of the facts that are behind the decisions that we make. We should be skeptical.
-*Dixy Lee Ray*

We need to be asking for the vote in the most powerful way possible, which is to have people asking for the vote who are comfortable and look like and sound like the people that we're asking for the vote from.
-*Karl Rove*

We ought to consider what is the end of government, before we determine which is the best form.
-*John Adams*

We should not allow the word 'democracy' to be utilized apologetically to represent the dictatorship of the exploiting classes.
-*Che Guevara*

We should stop going around babbling about how we're the greatest democracy on earth, when we're not even a democracy. We are a sort of militarized republic. The founding fathers hated two things, one was monarchy and the other was democracy, they gave us a constitution that saw to it we will have neither. I don't know how wise they were.
-*Gore Vidal*

We still proclaim the old ideals of liberty but we cannot voice them without anxiety in our hearts. The question is no longer one of establishing democratic institutions but of preserving them.
-*Charles Evans Hughes*

We used to say in the White House that if a place is too dangerous, too small or too poor, send the First Lady.
-*Hillary Rodham Clinton*

We used to think that secrecy was perhaps the greatest enemy of democracy, and as long as there was no suppression or censorship, people could be trusted to make the informed decisions that would preserve our free society, but we have learned in recent years that the techniques of misinformation and misdirection have become so refined that, even in an open society, a cleverly directed flood of misinformation can overwhelm the truth, even though the truth is out there, uncensored, quietly available to anyone who can find it.
-*Daniel Dennett*

We want to be in control of our lives. Whether we are jungle fighters, craftsmen, company men, gamesmen, we want to be in control. And when the government erodes that control, we are not comfortable.
-*Barbara Jordan*

We who advocate peace are becoming an irrelevance when we speak peace. The government speaks rubber bullets, live bullets, tear gas, police dogs, detention, and death.
-*Desmond Tutu*

We who are liberal and progressive know that the poor are our equals in every sense except that of being equal to us.
-*Lionel Trilling*

We will create a civilization of the Mind in Cyberspace. May it be more humane and fair than the world your governments have made before.
-*John Perry Barlow*

We will not be intimidated or pushed off the world stage by people who do not like what we stand for, and that is, freedom, democracy and the fight against disease, poverty and terrorism.
-*Madeleine Albright*

We'd all like to vote for the best man, but he's never a candidate.
-*Frank McKinney (Kin) Hubbard*

We're a democratic society. Shutting down the government should not be on the agenda.
-*Alan Greenspan*

We're changing the Constitution out of fear. We spend all our time looking up each other's dresses. Fear's the only issue the Republican Party has. Vote for them, or the terrorists will win.
-*Merle Haggard*

We're in the hands of the state legislature and God, but at the moment, the state legislature has more to say than God.
-*Ed Koch*

We're more than just politicians. We're more than just the cynical, venal, narrow, corrupt profession that all too often is a reflection of the current culture. We are in fact the inheritors and the lifeblood of freedom.
-*Newt Gingrich*

We're no longer officially a superpower. Please turn in your badges.
-*Rachel Maddow*

The Big Book of American Political Quotations

We're not going to have the America that we want until we elect leaders who are going to tell the truth- not most days, but every day.
-Ann Richards

We've got to clear some of the room out of the prisons so we can put the bad guys in there, like the pedophiles and the politicians.
-Kinky Friedman

We've upped our standards. Up yours. (Presidential campaign slogan)
-Pat Paulsen

Welcome to the U.S. Capitol: Watch for falling expectations.
-Wiley Miller

Well, sure, the government lies, and the newspapers lie. But in a democracy, they aren't the same lies.
-Alexis A. Gilliland

Well, there doesn't seem anything else for an ex-President to do but to go into the country and raise big pumpkins.
-Chester A. Arthur

Well, they finally stopped us from sending marines to every war that we could hear of. They are having one in Afghanistan. The thing will be over before Congress can pronounce it, much less find out where it is located.
-Will Rogers

Well, when the President does it, that means it is not illegal.
-Richard M. Nixon

Were it left to me to decide whether we should have a government without newspapers or newspapers without a government, I should not hesitate a moment to prefer the latter.
-Thomas Jefferson

What Democratic congressmen do to their women staffers, Republican congressmen do to the country.
-Bill Maher

What are the American ideals? They are the development of the individual for his own and the common good; the development of the individual through liberty, and the attainment of the common good through democracy and social justice.
-Louis Brandeis

What art needs is greater men, and what politics needs is better men.
-William Saroyan

What becomes of our democracy when such conditions of inequality as these can be brought about through chicanery, he open violation of the law and defiance of the Constitution?
-James Weldon Johnson

What difference does it make to the dead, the orphans, and the homeless, whether the mad destruction is wrought under the name of totalitarianism or the holy name of liberty and democracy?
-Mohandas K. Gandhi

What do I believe in? Belief means faith, and there's only one damn thing in the world I have any faith in. That's the idea of American democracy, because it seems to me so obvious that that's the only sensible way to run human affairs.
-Rex Stout

What do you want me to do? I'm surrounded by a bunch of idiots. And democracy...
-*Indira Gandhi*

What does an actor know about politics?
-*Ronald Reagan*

What does the term 'anti-American' mean? Does it mean you are anti-jazz? Or that you're opposed to freedom of speech? That you don't delight in Toni Morrison or John Updike? That you have a quarrel with giant sequoias? Does it mean that you don't admire the hundreds of thousands of American citizens who marched against nuclear weapons, or the thousands of war resisters who forced their government to withdraw from Vietnam? Does it mean that you hate all Americans?
-*Arundhati Roy*

What else do conservatives and libertarians profess in common? The answer to that question is simple: nothing. Nor will they ever. To talk of forming a league or coalition between these two is like advocating a union of ice and fire.
-*Russell Kirk*

What experience and history teach is this- that nations and governments have never learned anything from history, or acted upon any lessons they might have drawn from it.
-*Georg Wilhelm Friedrich Hegel*

What is government but an arrangement by which the many accept the authority of the few?
-*Barbara Tuchman*

What is morally wrong cannot be politically right.
-*William Gladstone*

What is most important for democracy is not that great fortunes should not exist, but that great fortunes should not remain in the same hands.
-*Alexis de Tocqueville*

What is needed in politics is not the ability to lie but rather the sensibility to know when, where, how and to whom to say things.
-*Vaclav Havel*

What is new is that environmentalism intensely illuminates the need to confront the corporate domain at its most powerful and guarded point- the exclusive right to govern the systems of production.
-*Barry Commoner*

What is patriotism but the love of the food one ate as a child?
-*Lin Yutang*

What is the use of being elected or re-elected unless you stand for something?
-*Grover Cleveland*

What keeps the democracy alive at all but the hatred of excellence; the desire of the base to see no head higher than their own?
-*Mary Renault*

What really troubles me is that democracy is getting a bad name because it is identified with imposition and occupation.
-*Madeleine Albright*

What right does Congress have to go around making laws just because they deem it necessary? (as Washington, DC mayor)
-*Marion S. Barry, Jr.*

What the American people want to see in their president is somebody who not necessarily can win every fight, but they want to see him stand up and fight for what he believes, take his case to the American people.
-*Bernie Sanders*

What the government is good at is collecting taxes, taking away your freedoms and killing people. It's not good at much else.
-*Tom Clancy*

What the liberal really wants is to bring about change which will not in any way endanger his position.
-*Stokely Carmichael*

What troubles me is not that movie stars run for office, but that they find it easy to get elected. It should be difficult. It should be difficult for millionaires, too.
-*Shana Alexander*

What Washington needs is adult supervision.
-*Barack Obama*

What we call a democratic society might be defined for certain purposes as one in which the majority is always prepared to put down a revolutionary minority.
-*Walter Lippmann*

What we need is a president who is at least twelve kinds of nerd, a nerd messiah to come along every four years, acquire the Secret Service code name Poindexter, install a Revenge of the Nerds screen saver on the Oval Office computer, and one by one decrypt our woes.
-*Sarah Vowell*

What's good economics is bad politics; what's bad economics is good politics.
-*Eugene W. Baer*

What's real in politics is what the voters decide is real.
-*Ben J. Wattenberg*

What's the real difference between Republicans and Democrats? Republicans will always take on people in the interest of power and good democrats will never fear to take on the power in the interests of people.
-*James Carville*

Whatever it is that the government does, sensible Americans would prefer that the government do it to somebody else. This is the idea behind foreign policy.
-*P.J. O'Rourke*

When 25 percent of the population believe the President should be impeached and 51 percent of the population believe in UFOs, you may or may not need a new President, but you definitely need a new population.
-*Harry Reasoner*

When Congress alters the federal balance, it must carefully consider the consequences of doing so.
-*Anthony Kennedy*

When Conservatives crusade against government while they are try-ing to be appointed to head the government, I think that's weird!
-*Rachel Maddow*

When I became 21, I decided that nobody learned anything about politics after the age of 21.
-*Grover Norquist*

When I die, I want to be buried in Chicago, so I can still be active in politics.
-*Charlie Rangel*

When I entered politics, I took the only downward turn you could take from journalism.
-*Jim Hightower*

When I ran for Class President in the sixth grade, we were told we couldn't promise something we couldn't do.
-*Paula Poundstone*

When I want to buy up any politicians I always find the anti-monopolist the most purchasable, they don't come so high.
-*William Henty Vanderbilt*

When I was a boy I was told that anybody could become President. I'm beginning to believe it.
-*Clarence Darrow*

When I was a small boy in Kansas, a friend of mine and I went fishing and as we sat there in the warmth of the summer afternoon on a river bank, we talked about what we wanted to do when we grew up. I told him that I wanted to be a real major league baseball player, a genuine professional like Honus Wagner. My friend said that he'd like to be president of the United States. Neither of us got our wish.
-*Dwight D. Eisenhower*

The Big Book of American Political Quotations

When a dog howls at the moon, we call it religion. When he barks at strangers, we call it patriotism.
-*Edward Abbey*

When a machine begins to run without human aid, it is time to scrap it- whether it be a factory or a government.
-*Alexander Chase*

When a man assumes leadership, he forfeits the right to mercy.
-*Gennaro Anguilo*

When a member of the House moves over to the Senate, he raises the IQ of both bodies.
-*Everett Dirksen*

When a nation's young men are conservative, its funeral bell is already rung.
-*Henry Ward Beecher*

When a new source of taxation is found it never means, in practice, that an old source is abandoned. It merely means that the politicians have two ways of milking the taxpayer where they had only one before.
-*H.L. Mencken*

When a party can't think of anything else they always fall back on lower taxes. It has a magic sound to a voter just like Fairyland is spoken of and dreamed of by children. But no child has ever seen it. Neither has any voter ever lived to see the day when his taxes were lowered.
-*Will Rogers*

When a politician changes his position it's sometimes hard to tell whether he has seen the light or felt the heat.
-Robert Fuoss

When a politician starts preaching, I tend to react the same way as when a preacher starts talking politics. I become very, very wary.
-Madeleine Albright

When a religion rather than reason dictates legislation, do not expect logic with your law.
-Hugh Hefner

When a thing defies physical law, there's usually politics involved.
-P.J. O'Rourke

When an unorganized mob runs amok, intimidates people and steals their possessions without regard for their property rights, it's called looting. When an organized mob runs amok, intimidates people and steals their possessions without regard for their property rights, it's called government.
-Garry Reed

When buying and selling are controlled by legislation, the first things to be bought and sold are legislators.
-P.J. O'Rourke

When forced to choose between big corporations and big government, you should never choose big government because whatever you don't like about the big corporations will also be present in big government, only worse, and with guns.
-Matt Walsh

The Big Book of American Political Quotations

When free discussion is denied, hardening of the arteries of democracy has set in, free institutions are but a lifeless form, and the death of the republic is at hand.
-*William Randolph Hearst*

When men in politics are together, testosterone poisoning makes them insane.
-*Peggy Noonan*

When mothers talk about the depression of the empty nest, they're not mourning the passing of all those wet towels on the floor, or the music that numbs your teeth, or even the bottle of capless shampoo dribbling down the shower drain. They're upset because they've gone from supervisor of a child's life to a spectator. It's like being the vice president of the United States.
-*Erma Bombeck*

When our government is spoken of as some menacing, threatening, foreign entity, it ignores the fact that in our democracy, government is us.
-*Barack Obama*

When people fear surveillance, whether it exists or not, they grow afraid to speak their minds and hearts freely to their government or to anyone else.
-*Samuel J. Ervin*

When philosophers try to be politicians they generally cease to be philosophers.
-*Walter Lippmann*

When political ammunition runs low, inevitably the rusty artillery of abuse is wheeled into action.
-*Adlai E. Stevenson II*

When politicians complain that TV turns proceedings into a circus, it should be made clear that the circus was already there, and that TV has merely demonstrated that not all the performers are well trained.
-*Edward R. Murrow*

When politicians say 'I'm in politics,' it may or may not be possible to trust them, but when they say, 'I'm in public service,' you know you should flee.
-*Albert Jay Nock*

When politics and religion are intermingled, a people is suffused with a sense of invulnerability, and gathering speed in their forward charge, they fail to see the cliff ahead of them.
-*Frank Herbert*

When somebody's muffler shop goes bankrupt, the government doesn't pay him $100,000 to not install mufflers.
-*P.J. O'Rourke*

When the Democrats form a firing squad, they stand in a circle.
-*Mort Sahl*

When the government gives things names, you should keep your sense of irony handy.
-*Joseph Sobran*

When the government puts its imprimatur on a particular religion it conveys a message of exclusion to all those who do not adhere to the favored beliefs. A government cannot be premised on the belief that all persons are created equal when it asserts that God prefers some.
-*Harry Blackmun*

When the government violates the people's rights, insurrection is, for the people and for each portion of the people, the most sacred of the rights and the most indispensible of duties.
-Marquis de Lafayette

When the leaders choose to make themselves bidders at an auction of popularity, their talents, in the construction of the state, will be of no service. They will become flatterers instead of legislators; the instruments, not the guides, of the people.
-Edmund Burke

When the political columnists say 'Every thinking man' they mean themselves, and when candidates appeal to 'Every intelligent voter' they mean everybody who is going to vote for them.
-Franklin P. Adams

When the search for truth is confused with political advocacy, the pursuit of knowledge is reduced to the quest for power.
-Alston Chase

When the sense of justice seeks to express itself quite outside the regular channels of established government, it has set forth on a dangerous journey inevitably ending in disaster.
-Jane Addams

When the three branches of government have failed to represent the citizenry and the mass of the media has failed to represent the citizenry, then the citizenry better represent the citizenry.
-David Mamet

When the tyrant has disposed of foreign enemies by conquest or treaty, and there is nothing to fear from them, then he is always stirring up some war or other, in order that the people may require a leader.
-*Plato*

When there is a lack of honor in government, the morals of the whole people are poisoned.
-*Herbert Hoover*

When they call the roll in the Senate, the Senators do not know whether to answer 'present' or 'not guilty.'
-*Theodore Roosevelt*

When threatened, the first thing a democracy gives up is democracy.
-*Mignon McLaughlin*

When too many Americans don't vote or participate, some see apathy and despair. I see disappointment and even outrage. And I believe that out of this frustration can come hope and action.
-*Paul Wellstone*

When we are sick, we want an uncommon doctor; when we have a construction job to do, we want an uncommon engineer, and when we are at war, we want an uncommon general. It is only when we get into politics that we are satisfied with the common man.
-*Herbert Hoover*

When women understand that governments and religions are human inventions; that Bibles, prayer-books, catechisms, and encyclical letters are all emanations from the brains of man, they will no longer be oppressed by the injunctions that come to them with the divine authority of 'Thus sayeth the Lord.'
-*Elizabeth Cady Stanton*

The Big Book of American Political Quotations

When you are right, you cannot be too radical; When you are wrong, you cannot be too conservative.
-*Rev. Martin Luther King, Jr.*

When you argue stupid, you campaign stupid. When you campaign stupid, you win stupid. And when you win stupid, you govern stupid.
-*David Frum*

When you get into politics, you find that all your worst nightmares about it turn out to be true, and the people who are attracted to large concentrations of power are precisely the ones who should be kept as far away from it as possible.
-*Ken Livingstone*

When you get to be President, there are all those things, the honors, the twenty-one gun salutes, all those things. You have to remember it isn't for you. It's for the Presidency.
-*Harry S. Truman*

When you say 'radical right' today, I think of these moneymaking ventures by fellows like Pat Robertson and others who are trying to take the Republican Party and make a religious organization out of it. If that ever happens, kiss politics goodbye.
-*Barry M. Goldwater*

When you're a performer, you have to please a large audience. And when you're in politics, you have to please a large audience, too.
-*Shirley Temple*

When you're the leader, everything is your fault.
-*Terry Goodkind*

When you've written to your President, to your congressman, to your senator and nothing, nothing has come of it, you take to the streets.
-Eric Bouza

When your opponent sets up a straw man, set it on fire and kick the cinders around the stage. Don't worry about losing the Strawperson-American community vote.
-James Lileks

When, in the late 1940s, we faced a global Cold War against another system of ideological fanatics certain that their authoritarian values would eventually rule the world, we prevailed in time. We prevailed because we exercised patience as well as vigilance, self-restraint as well as self-defense, and reached out to moderates and modernists, to democrats and dissidents, within that closed system.
-Theodore (Ted) Sorensen

Whenever a fellow tells me he is bipartisan, I know he's going to vote against me.
-Harry S. Truman

Whenever is found what is called a paternal government, there is found state education. It has been discovered that the best way to ensure implicit obedience is to commence tyranny in the nursery.
-Benjamin Disraeli

Whenever the government of the United States shall break up, it will probably be in consequence of a false direction having been given to public opinion.
-James Fenimore Cooper

Whenever the legislature attempts to regulate the differences between masters and their workmen, its counsellors are always the masters. When the regulation, therefore, is in favor of the workmen, it is always just and equitable; but it is sometimes otherwise when in favor of the masters.
-Adam Smith

Where a government has come into power through some form of popular vote... the guerrilla outbreak cannot be promoted, since the possibilities of peaceful struggle have not yet been exhausted.
-Che Guevara

Where is the politician who has not promised to fight to the death for lower taxes- and who has not proceeded to vote for the very spending projects that make tax cuts impossible?
-Barry M. Goldwater

Where mass opinion dominates the government, there is a morbid derangement of the true functions of power. The derangement brings about the enfeeblement, verging on paralysis, of the capacity to govern. This breakdown in the constitutional order is the cause of the precipitate and catastrophic decline of Western society.
-Walter Lippmann

Where there is a sufficient social movement of self-reliant communities, there can be political change. There must be political change.
-Jerry Brown

Where there is politics or economics, there is no morality.
-Karl Wilhelm Friedrich Schlegel

Wherever, in any country the whole people feel that the happiness of all is dependent upon the happiness of the weakest, there freedom exists.
-*Booker T. Washington*

Wherever the real power in a Government lies, there is the danger of oppression.
-*James Madison*

Wherever you have an efficient government you have a dictatorship.
-*Harry S. Truman*

Wherever you see a man who gives someone else's corruption, someone else's prejudice as a reason for not taking action himself, you see a cog in The Machine that governs us.
-*John Jay Chapman*

Whether a man is burdened by power or enjoys power; whether he is trapped by responsibility or made free by it; whether he is moved by other people and outer forces or moves them- this is of the essence of leadership.
-*Theodore H. White*

Whether it comes from a despotic sovereign or an elected president, from a murderous general or a beloved leader, I see power as an inhuman and hateful phenomenon.
-*Oriana Fallaci*

Whether ours shall continue to be a government of laws and not of men is now for Congress and ultimately the American people to decide.
-*Archibald Cox*

While all other Sciences have advanced, that of Government is at a stand; little better understood; little better practiced now than three or four thousand years ago.
-John Adams

While democracy in the long run is the most stable form of government, in the short run, it is among the most fragile.
-Madeleine Albright

While democracy must have its organizations and controls, its vital breath is individual liberty.
-Charles Evans Hughes

White Americans have a very unusual sense of history. They make it up as they go along, constantly revising to suit their tastes in a manner that would make Stalin blush. Very few of them saw any irony in the fact that during a recent nasty Balkans conflict, when Uncle Sam intervened to stop the Serbs from ethnically cleansing the Bosnians, the military action was performed using Apache helicopter gunships. Helicopters named after a people that had been ethnically cleansed in the United States less than one hundred years previously. Sixteen lane highways across the sacred burial grounds. Yee-hah.
-Craig Ferguson

White collar conservative flashin down the street, pointing that plastic finger at me, they all assume my kind will drop and die, but I'm gonna wave my freak flag high.
-Jimi Hendrix

Who is wise? He that learns from everyone. Who is powerful? He that governs his passions. Who is rich? He that is content. Who is that? Nobody.
-Benjamin Franklin

Why do the people humiliate themselves by voting? I didn't vote because I have dignity. If I had closed my nose and voted for one of them, I would spit on my own face.
-Oriana Fallaci

Why has government been instituted at all? Because the passions of men will not conform to the dictates of reason and justice, without constraint.
-Alexander Hamilton

Why is this soiled, crumpled, overdecorated piece of paper bearing a picture of a rather disreputable president worth fifty dollars, while this clean, soft, white, and cleverly folded piece of paper is worth so little that I just wiped my nose on it?
-P.J. O'Rourke

Why take a chance on a candidate who might lose? You can always buy them after the election.
-Santo Trafficante, Jr.

Will people ever be wise enough to refuse to follow bad leaders or to take away the freedom of other people?
-Eleanor Roosevelt

Wisdom and good governance require more than the consistent application of abstract principles.
-Theodore Dalrymple

Wisdom is essential in a president, the appearance of wisdom will do in a candidate.
-Eric Sevareid

With all its faults, the American political system is the freest and most democratic in the world.
-Eldridge Cleaver

With exceptions so rare they are regarded as miracles of nature, successful democratic politicians are insecure and intimidated men.
-Walter Lippmann

With perfect citizens any Government is good.
-Stephen Leacock

With the end of the nominating process, American politics leaves logic behind.
-Theodore H. White

With words we govern men.
-Benjamin Disraeli

Without alienation, there can be no politics.
-Arthur Miller

Without faith we might relapse into scientific or rational thinking, which leads by a slippery slope toward constitutional democracy.
-Robert Anton Wilson

Women are early taught that to appear to yield is the only way to govern.
-Sarah Moore Grimke

Women have a lot to say about how to advance women's rights, and governments need to learn from that, listen to the movement and respond.
-Charlotte Bunch

The Big Book of American Political Quotations

World War II was the last government program that really worked.
-*George F. Will*

Would it not be more economical for the governments to build asylums for the sane instead of the demented?
-*Kahlil Gibran*

Writing laws is easy, but governing is difficult.
-*Leo Tolstoy*

Years ago, fairy tales all began with 'Once upon a time...' Now we know they all begin with 'If I am elected.'
-*Carolyn Warner*

Yet in all our rejoicing let us neither express, nor cherish, any harsh feeling towards any citizen who, by his vote, has differed with us. Let us at all times remember that all American citizens are brothers of a common country, and should dwell together in the bonds of fraternal feeling.
-*Abraham Lincoln*

You are 'free' only in one sense: free from education in governing your life yourself, free from self-criticism.
-*Wilhelm Reich*

You are not to inquire how your trade may be increased, nor how you are to become a great and powerful people, but how your liberties can be secured; for liberty ought to be the direct end of your Government.
-*Patrick Henry*

You are smarter than the government, so when the government pays you to do something you wouldn't do on your own, it is almost always paying you to do something stupid.
-*P.J. O'Rourke*

You begin saving the world by saving one man at a time; all else is grandiose romanticism or politics.
-*Charles Bukowski*

You campaign in poetry. You govern in prose.
-*Mario Cuomo*

You can choose whatever name you like for the two types of government. I personally call the type of government which can be removed without violence 'democracy', and the other 'tyranny.'
-*Karl Popper*

You can never have a revolution in order to establish a democracy. You must have a democracy in order to have a revolution.
-*G.K. Chesterton*

You can question somebody's views and their judgment without questioning their motives or patriotism.
-*Barack Obama*

You can talk about capitalism and communism and all that sort of thing, but the important thing is the struggle everybody is engaged in to get better living conditions, and they are not interested too much in government.
-*Bernard Baruch*

You can tell a lot about a politician's goals by noticing who he wants to keep stirred-up and angry, and who he doesn't.
-*Glenn Reynolds*

You can't be a full participant in our democracy if you don't know our history.
-*David McCullough*

You can't do progressive government from the inside. You have to rally those outsiders and make them a force.
-Jim Hightower

You can't ignore politics, no matter how much you'd like to.
-Molly Ivins

You cannot be a leader, and ask other people to follow you, unless you know how to follow, too.
-Sam Rayburn

You cannot govern, you cannot administrate, with an ignoramus.
-Oriana Fallaci

You cannot manage a man into combat; you must lead him. You manage things, you lead people. We went overboard on management and forgot about leadership.
-Admiral Grace Murray Hopper

You cannot preach self-government and liberty to people in a starving land.
-Fiorello LaGuardia

You do not examine legislation in the light of the benefits it will convey if properly administered, but in the light of the wrongs it would do and the harms it would cause if improperly administered.
-Lyndon B. Johnson

You do not lead by hitting people over the head. That's assault, not leadership.
-Dwight D. Eisenhower

You don't really know what to believe until the Government denies it.
-*Brian Wilson*

You don't spread democracy through the barrel of a gun.
-*Helen Thomas*

You don't tell us how to stage the news, and we don't tell you how to report it. (as press secretary for President George W. Bush)
-*Larry Speakes*

You have achieved excellence as a leader when people will follow you anywhere, if only out of curiosity.
-*Colin Powell*

You have the army of mediocrities followed by the multitude of fools. As the mediocrities and the fools always form the immense majority, it is impossible for them to elect an intelligent government.
-*Guy de Maupassant*

You have to be careful as a libertarian because you can sound very Republican.
-*Penn Jillette*

You have to have a certain realism that government is a pretty blunt instrument and without the constant attention of highly qualified people with the right metrics, it will fall into not doing things very well.
-*Bill Gates*

You have to have been a Republican to know how good it is to be a Democrat.
-*Jacqueline Kennedy Onassis*

You have to live among rich liberals to understand what they're saying. You'll never believe what they mean by 'middle class.' They mean themselves.
-*Joel Stein*

You know I could run for governor but I'm basically a media creation. I've never done anything. I've worked for my dad. I worked in the oil business. But that's not the kind of profile you have to have to get elected to public office. (In 1989)
-*George W. Bush*

You know the one group I never criticize? Politicians. Politicians are put there by the public. Garbage in, garbage out. You get the leadership you deserve.
-*George Carlin*

You know, I think many people have the mistaken impression that Congress regulates Wall Street. In truth that's not the case. The real truth is that Wall Street regulates the Congress.
-*Bernie Sanders*

You know, sometimes, when they say you are ahead of your time, it's just a polite way of saying you have a real bad sense of timing.
-*George McGovern*

You learn far more from negative leadership than from positive leadership. Because you learn how not to do it. And, therefore, you learn how to do it.
-*H. Norman Schwartzkopf, Jr.*

You live in a democracy. You don't work in one.
-*Douglas Dahlberg*

You measure democracy by the freedom it gives its dissidents, not the freedom it gives its assimilated conformists.
-*Abbie Hoffman*

You must not give power to a man unless, above everything else, he has character. Character is the most important qualification the President of the United States can have.
-*Richard M. Nixon*

You need to understand something, you drink deeply from wells of freedom and liberty and opportunity that you did not dig. You eat lavishly from banquet tables prepared for you by your ancestors. You sit under the shade of trees that you did not plant or cultivate or care for. You have a choice in life, you can just sit back, getting fat, dumb, and happy, consuming all the blessings put before you, or it can metabolize inside of you, become fuel to get you into the fight, to make this democracy real, to make it true to its words that we can be a nation of liberty and justice for all.
-*Cory Booker*

You say we (reporters) are distracting from the business of government. Well, I hope so. Distracting a politician from governing is like distracting a bear from eating your baby.
-*P.J. O'Rourke*

You show me ten men who cherish some religious doctrine or political ideology, and I'll show you nine men whose minds are utterly impervious to any factual evidence which contradicts their beliefs, and who regard the producer of such evidence as a criminal who ought to be suppressed.
-*H. Beam Piper*

You take your classified telephone directory, and open up 'Churches', and have a ruler in your hand. And you will find that the longest space is occupied by authoritarian, Bible-banging churches. And these people are barbarians, who take the written word of the Bible literally. Because they need terribly, they have a personal need, for something to depend on.... The government realizes that there is a very large number of people like that; and therefore, to keep their votes, they have to pander to those kind of people. And these are the boys who never grew up; they always need Papa.... The trouble is that the boys who need Papa, are violent. They have the guns. And they are the types of people who like to be soldiers, policemen- tough guys. And therefore they have a great deal of power.
-Alan Watts

You tell me your favorite novelists and I'll tell you whom you vote for, or whether you vote at all.
-Stephen Vizinczey

You will find that you cannot do without politicians. They are a necessary evil in this day and time.
-Huey P. Long

You will never escape the will of the mob. About the best anyone has ever figured out to do is herd them into voting booths.
-Barry Shein

You'll never have a quiet world till you knock the patriotism out of the human race.
-George Bernard Shaw

You're not supposed to be so blind with patriotism that you can't face reality. Wrong is wrong, no matter who says it.
-Malcolm X

You've got to be optimist to be a Democrat, and you've got to be a humorist to stay one.
-*Will Rogers*

You've got to pity the poor Democrats in Congress. Most of them are on record against capital punishment, since they naturally don't want to diminish their constituent base.
-*Wes Pruden*

You've really got to wear a chastity belt in Washington to preserve your journalistic virginity. Once the secretary of state invites you to lunch and asks your opinion, you're sunk.
-*I.F. Stone*